The Gift of Courage is a powerf
of inspiring stories of courageous
happiness while helping heal the world.

—MARCI SHIMOFF
#1 *NY Times* Bestselling Author, *Happy for No Reason, Love for No Reason,*
and *Chicken Soup for the Woman's Soul*

This book is a reminder to us all that our finest moments are when we take those courageous risks to stand up to bullies or take risks on others' behalf. In a world where we are often disappointed in the lack of courage in our national and local political leaders, *The Gift of Courage* is a respite. We see the difference everyday heroes can make in the lives of others. The reporting here is solid and the inspiration profound.

—GERALDINE LAYBOURNE
Former President of Nickelodeon and Founder of the Oxygen Network

Kelley's story is one that anyone can take to heart, no matter what your particular challenge. The inspiring and honest telling of how she managed to come to a deeper, fuller appreciation of the gift of living is one of the good news stories that resonate within every life.

—MERYL STREEP
Academy Award-winning actress

Ken Streater has created a collection of real-life stories that not only grip your mind and heart, they uplift and inspire you. *The Gift of Courage* is a gem. I'm personally better for having spent time with it, and you will be too. Read this book and you will be changed.

—ROGER SEIP
Author of the best-selling book *Train Your Brain for Success*

In *The Gift of Courage* Ken Streater has compiled a valuable reminder that there are among us, in our everyday lives, those who have faced life-crushing challenges and used the experience to better the world around them.

—LYNN SCHOOLER
Award-winning author of *The Blue Bear* and *Walking Home*

THE GIFT OF
COURAGE

To the clients and friends
of Jonathan of CSSI —

I ENJOY SERVING YOU BOB.
THE AUTHOR OF THIS BOOK,
IS A GOOD FRIEND OF MINE.
ENJOY! WARMEST
REGARDS

23.10.14

THE GIFT OF
COURAGE

STORIES OF
OPEN HEARTS
PASSION AND
PURPOSE

KEN STREATER

TABLE OF CONTENTS

To Leo Durand,

the most courageous and giving person I know.
No one is better than you at going with the flow
and knowing when to take a powerful stand.

INTRODUCTION

Faced with what is right, to leave it undone shows a lack
of courage.

— CONFUCIUS

Courage is the price that life exacts for granting peace.

— AMELIA EARHART

Those who know "why they are here" may tell you they
have always known it—or that it just came to them one
day. Others are just naturally generous and fulfilled and do
not even ponder the meaning of their lives. Some did not easily uncover life's purpose but ultimately found it by opening
their hearts. I belong to this group. But for many, the search
continues. This journey takes courage, and once your meaning is realized the rewards are magnificent and infinite.

The meaning of the word "courage" is "of the heart." There
are three types of courage: instant, assumed, and deep. Instant
courage benefits others as an act of spontaneous bravery or
giving, when a life is on the line, danger roars in as a here-and-
now circumstance, or someone suffers in front of you. Think
of saving a child from drowning, pushing someone away from
a careening car, or just instinctively giving a hand, a hug, or a
shoulder to cry on. These acts are from the heart even while
you are not conscious of it in the moment.

Emergency personnel, adventure guides, leading athletes, soldiers, community and business leaders, and others who regularly place themselves in harmful or high-pressure situations exemplify assumed courage. It is both innate and developed through experience, and it is consistently available for members of this rare group to draw upon. This courage is an act of the heart and of the will.

Deep courage focuses on self. It is taking time to understand what truly matters to you, giving energy to rediscover your passions, and having the guts to kindly expose your heart—to yourself and to the world. This is the self-inspired courage that emboldens you to uncover and embrace your "why." Finding your life's purpose requires an open heart.

The Gift of Courage is about regular yet extraordinary people who use courage—instant, assumed, and deep—to live passionate and purposeful lives. They are changing our world. Some realize their purpose through searing experiences far beyond what most of us will ever endure. Others uncover it through prolonged introspection. The rest find it in a moment of chance. In every case these common heroes give from the heart. Their lives of purpose are gifts that radiate goodness and lift the universe. This is *the gift of courage.*

Here are stories of lifechangers, lifemakers, and lifesavers. It is likely you have never heard of any of them. They could be your neighbor or might live half a world away. Each has unique characteristics that embolden them with courage to live a meaningful life by serving others, an impact which permeates the bounds of space and time. Please meet:

Jim Adams, a devout fireman who was baked alive and survived through technology, grace, and a need to serve a greater cause. Conviction in his beliefs and commitment to a community of firefighters and burn survivors enables Jim to lead a rich, passionate life as he did before and since surviving an accident in which most others would have died.

Kelley Kalafatich, a pioneer world-class river guide who helped create a new third-world economy, worked to preserve wild rivers, inspired hundreds of young women to live their dreams, and who is now hoping to walk again. Kelley's determination in the face of a life-altering illness illustrates the power of facing fears to realize a life of purpose.

Josh Kern, a white law school student who challenged the stigma of hopelessness in a violent black inner-city neighborhood with Thurgood Marshall Academy, a charter high school where every single graduate advances to college as a future leader. Josh empowers hundreds of at-risk children and young adults with confidence to pursue their dreams.

Martha Ryan, a care-giving program founder, along with former homeless mothers Judy Crawford and Carrie Hamilton, who now use their past hardships to help build bright futures for those who live on the streets. Their collective stories showcase how acceptance and self-forgiveness are necessary to serve others well.

Jeff Leeland, a teacher whose students raised money to save his son's life, and who built an organization from that experience to save hundreds more lives and unexpectedly, his own.

Jeff's compassion for others and himself reveals the cornerstone of a passion-filled life.

Dennis Guthrie, a highly decorated Vietnam War hero who buried his emotions during the war to save hundreds of lives and now shares them freely to save thousands more. Dennis' devotion to fellow soldiers at times of war and peace empower him and countless others to survive the literal and emotional hell of war.

Brianna Mercado, a teenage cancer survivor who lost a precious year of her life fighting the disease. Now a young college student, she gives very ill children reasons to live through the gift of dance and laughter. With uncommon wisdom, Brianna teaches us how resilience—getting back up—is vital to joy and generosity.

Eric Plantenberg, a personal development leader who inspires people to realize their own personal summits, as he did by climbing Mt. Everest to raise money for children's education in Pakistan and Afghanistan. Eric's life and teachings spotlight introspection as a gateway to courage and an abundant life.

This book is woven with a thread of gratitude for opportunities, mentors, community members, and life itself. As I set out on this book's journey, I had one friend in mind: Kelley Kalafatich. I wanted to tell Kelley's story and to help her in the same way she has helped so many, including me. Nearly thirty years ago in a quiet African hut, Kelley and other dear friends gave me great comfort through a night of deep despair when I received news that my father had unexpectedly died back home. I am grateful for the positive impact of compassionate people, as are others who are changed by Kelley and these other brave people.

To learn more about the character and impact of courage, I scoured the country. I found valiant, purpose-driven people in the inner city, the backwoods, and everywhere else in the fabric of America. For some, I had to look no further than my own community. People living their dreams are everywhere.

Courage is born of a simple desire to do the right thing. It forms when action is taken, even in the face of challenge or risk. Whether putting your life on the line or stepping just outside your comfort zone, risk is relative. Acting on your belief is not; it is required. *This is courage.* When a person accepts and embraces challenge and then takes action—by spontaneous demand or intentional dealings with personal fears—their unique greatness is revealed and shared with the world.

Those touched by purposeful people often pay forward that energy to another person or to their communities. Once in the world, courage spreads and multiplies forever. Courage always moves on. At Washington D.C.'s Thurgood Marshall Academy, teachers inspire achievement in the face of adversity. Students learn by their example and bring that knowledge and character into the world. The courageous uplift those around them, anytime, anywhere.

In this book, the term community is used loosely. It can be a group of firefighters, soldiers, river guides, or students; it is an organization or a cause. Your reading of this book forms a new community. Portions from the sale of *The Gift of Courage* go to the people, families, or organizations described in this book. These donations help to cover rehabilitation expenses and fund nonprofits associated with their stories. By purchasing this book you are rewarding those deserving of recognition.

An old proverb states that gifts are meant to travel. Just knowing that these people make the world better could inspire you to be courageous and to act on what matters most. Thank you for taking time by reading these pages to discover the beauty of open hearts, the joy of caring, the meaning of purpose, and the gift of courage. Thank you for being a part of this community.

Note: This book is not a how-to manual on deep courage. That book is *The Courage Compass: An Essential Guide to Finding Your Meaning and Purpose.* In *The Courage Compass*, notable people and I will share what we've learned in coming to know our purpose. Those insights and tools are offered to help you on your journey of finding your "why." See *The Courage Compass* website (www.thecouragecompass.com) for more information.

JIM ADAMS

Conviction

The opposite of life is not death, it is indifference.
— ELIE WIESEL

I believe it means we are all one. There is unity among
all things and every woman and man is the child of God.
— JIM ADAMS, on THE SHEMA

Jim's skin came off in Nate Damiano's hands. It was just after midnight, the start of New Year's Day 2010, when the fire truck from Station Five in Modesto, California pulled up to the burning house on Coston Avenue. None of the men onboard expected the truck's engineer, Jim Adams, or firefighter J.D. Clevenger to become the next casualties of the economic downturn that left cities across the nation studded with foreclosed and derelict homes. Since the collapse in 2008, the number of people living below the poverty level in Modesto skyrocketed. Though scavengers had torn most of the home's wiring out, a needy family still rented the house. They were using a small generator to power a heater with an electric cord run into the house from the garage. When the mother of the family lit a candle for light to refill the generator's fuel tank, fumes from gas cans stored in the garage ignited. Within minutes of receiving the alarm call, the men of Station Five suited up in the heavy, fire-resistant coats and pants designed to withstand thousand-degree temperatures, and the trucks were rolling.

Jim, J.D., and Station Captain Greg Ewert were among the first on the scene. The captain of a fire engine from another station that arrived moments earlier shouted to them what he knew of the fire's origin in the garage. Nate Damiano, a member of the Rapid Intervention Crew (RIC), pulled up in a rig from a third station. Under most circumstances RICs do not engage a fire, but are present only to act as rescuers of the men who are actively fighting the blaze.

While Damiano and the rest of the RIC readied their gear, Jim, J.D., and Captain Ewert placed a ladder against the house to reach the roof. With the interior of the garage engulfed in flames, the best way to control the inferno was to cut a vent in the roof directly over the worst of it. This allows the heat and fire to escape upward to prevent conditions inside the garage from exploding into a deadly "flashover" fire.

Jim and J.D. quickly checked each other's safety gear and started up the ladder. J.D. was carrying a chainsaw in his hand. Captain Ewert, coming behind, paused at the top of the ladder to change the frequency on his hand-held radio as Jim and J.D. eased out onto the roof of the garage. Jim probed for dangerous weak spots with his roof hook, a heavy two-pronged rake with a fiberglass handle. Reaching the ridgeline, Jim indicated the best spot for J.D. to saw a vent and stepped back as J.D. yanked the chainsaw to life.

At that moment the roof collapsed.

Captain Ewert, with one foot on the roof and the other still on the ladder, yelled a mayday into his radio as Jim and J.D. fell into the flames. Jim landed hard on his knees with burning debris showering down on him, then rolled onto his left side with his left arm instinctively raised to protect his face. J.D., swept down with the collapse, landed on his feet but fell to his hands and knees in the inferno.

"I hit the chainsaw brake and tried to throw it off to the side as we started to fall," said J.D. later. "We fell sixteen feet down and hit hard on a mountain of junk, years of squatters' crap all around us." There were car tires, cabinets, old stereos, and books, all on fire. "Then everything went black," said J.D. "Completely black. The collapsing roof created a vacuum of smoke and I could not see a thing. I knew I was on fire."

J.D. heard Captain Ewert yelling the mayday call as he dropped into the flames. He saw Jim fall to his right and tried to scurry up a burning rafter to the opening overhead, breaking through a layer of roofing material. "Then I heard Jim scream," he continued, "and I fell back into the heart of the fire."

Surrounded by fire and debris, J.D. struggled to find a way out to save himself and Jim. "I knew there was going to be a man-door from the garage into the house, and one that led outside," J.D. continued. "Since I fell closest to the house and had a sense of where that door might be I began crawling as fast as I could through a bunch of crap. I could not tell what I was crawling through. I came to something solid and thought that it might be fallen roof material."

Smoke and flame made it impossible for J.D. to see. He tried to punch his way toward the door. "I swung my ax to get through the debris. I smashed into it ten or fifteen times as I felt my skin burning. I began to think I was not going to survive. My skin was chalking, searing, burning. A billion things went through my mind. I had a distinct image of my wife and son holding hands in front of me. I really wanted to see them again. I kept pounding and pounding and pounding."

Then a spray of water from a fire hose directed at the blaze from somewhere outside the garage hit him. Understanding immediately that pushing into the hose stream would lead him out of the burning garage, he rolled to the side and crawled back the way he came to find Jim in the flames and smoke.

"It was like looking through the small wood-burning stove window into nothing but fire and char," he explained. "At that point the power of the fire was overwhelming. I could feel it rushing, pulsing, and vibrating all around me. My instincts said 'just run away.'"

He heard Jim scream and stopped, holding his breath and closing his eyes to see if he could pinpoint Jim's location by the direction of his screams. After a moment, he yelled "We're coming, Jim! Where are you? Keep making noise!" and started to crawl again.

"Then I felt a strange feeling on my face," J.D. continued, "like a deflating balloon. It was my mask melting into my face. My inhaling caused the overheated air mask to collapse against my skin."

J.D. had no time left. He turned around and clawed his way back toward the hose stream, crawling until he hit something he recognized as a washing machine. "I knew I was close to the wall against the house," said J.D., "so I crawled around the washing machine to the left, which was just a lucky guess."

When he saw two faint glowing points in the gloom, he recognized them as the LED lights of a member of the RIC team who ran into the house at Ewert's mayday call. J.D. ran past the rescuer and into the hall, ripping off his melting mask and yelling "Jim is still inside! Jim is still inside!"

Jim was in deep trouble. Firefighters' jackets and pants—called "turnouts"—keep their integrity in fires over 1,000 degrees, but masks are only good to around 425 degrees. Jim knew his weak link was his face. With flames engulfing him, and with the heat in the garage approaching several hundred degrees, he could feel different portions of his body baking. The back of his legs and buttocks were burning, dying, even though the flames had not fully breached his turnout. Another minute now lost in the inferno, he continued to protect his face with his left arm, but as he did the heat exploded through his jacket sleeve and glove. As he worked to free himself, his right arm also started to burn. Without the use of his hand, he was unable to use his radio and could not move.

Outside, J.D. burst out of the fire into the adjoining kitchen and then reached the yard. He and Captain Ewert ran to the main garage door and ripped it down, raking and pulling the debris out of the way with their fire hooks. Once the garage door was down, Captain Ewert fought his way into the burn to reach Jim. J.D. was close behind when another firefighter wrestled him to the ground, yelling that he was still on fire.

"I just wanted to get back to Jim," said J.D. "My friends dragged me away from the building toward the lawn, and as I was moved away from the house I could see the flames still shooting fifteen to twenty feet above the top of the garage walls, flashing over the structure."

J.D. ripped off his hood while others pulled off his jacket and pants to decrease the temperature against his body. The rescuers wrapped him in a burn blanket and surveyed his injuries.

Meanwhile, Captain Ewert moved deeper into the heat and smoke. Nate and Scott Hall, another member of the RIC, entered through the burning doorway between the kitchen and the garage. Scott and Nate knew Jim might be dead, but still powered deep into the inferno, shoving aside burning timbers in a blanket of dark smoke and flames. At last, they heard Jim's screams and struggled toward his voice in a mass of burning rubble.

Nate reached Jim first, moved in front of him, and shouted that they were going to get him out. At the same time Captain Ewert, coming from the opposite direction, reached through the smoke and felt a firefighter's arm. Scott wedged himself behind Jim and secured a hold under Jim's armpits as Nate grasped Jim's legs behind each thigh to lift them to his shoulders. With their faces inches apart, Nate heard Jim speaking or even praying, but in a language Nate did not understand.

Several years earlier Jim traveled to Israel to learn more about the Old Testament and Judaism. The prayer he muttered was the Shema, the traditional last words spoken by Jews facing death. Jim recited Deuteronomy 6:4 in Hebrew—"Sh'ma Yis'ra'eil Adonai Eloheinu Adonai echad"—meaning "Hear, Israel, the Lord is our God, the Lord is One."

For most of his life Jim was a seeker. Even as a child he questioned virtually everything to find answers. The curiosity and questioning continued into adulthood. He seldom explored questions of religion or spirituality and was a self-titled "Christmas and Easter Christian" until his thirties when he discovered his own personal God.

Jim questioned the essence of the New Testament and the Christian Bible and explored other religions to understand those beliefs. He found the Old Testament and Judaism and learned Hebrew to personally interpret the word. Jim traveled to Israel to study the history and culture of a path he found compelling and ultimately converted to Judaism.

For over a quarter century, Jim Adams fought fires for Modesto Fire Department and lived in the Sierra Nevada foothill hamlet of Angels Camp, twenty miles east of Modesto. Jim and his wife Amy raised a family on twenty acres, first for a couple of years in a manufactured home and then in a home of simple country elegance they built from the ground up. Countless evenings on the front deck brought sweeping views, privacy, and peace of mind to Jim and Amy. Their open space slopes quietly toward Yosemite and the grand Sierra Nevada peaks. Their two sons are grown now, with children of their own.

With thousands of calls under his belt, Jim approached his job intensely. Whether catastrophic warehouse fires, tragic car accidents, or burning duplexes, for over two decades Jim took care of Modesto night and day, earning the praise and gratitude of colleagues and community members alike. And he never grew complacent. After a call he took aside novice firefighters and discussed the way they approached a fire: what went right, what went wrong, what they could do better next time.

Jim would then put on gym clothes and invite station mates to join him in a workout. If the invitation went unanswered, he headed to the gym on his own. Upon his return, sweating but not winded, he checked the grease fittings on his truck, shined up the plated steel along its sides, and made sure the truck's dozens of tools were correctly in place. As the sun set, he would sit down with six other guys over plates of lasagna, say a prayer, laugh about how lasagna *is* kosher, and call it a night.

Jim quit the firefighters' union and was the only full-fledged fireman in Modesto not a member. He felt it was too politicized and lost sight of its true purpose: to help protect working firemen in terms of wages, benefits, and other employment-related concerns. He thought the unions were too focused on elections, with causes that he did not support, and political persuasions that seemed far removed from human resource issues.

Firehouses around the country each have distinct personalities, courtesy of the firefighters who staff them. Choosing to work at Modesto's Station Five, living and working with Jim and Captain Ewert, meant being challenged and supported without compromise. "Jim was so knowledgeable, had very high expectations, and he lived by example. Jim was demanding of himself and he would call others out on their mistakes,"

J.D. explained. "I was afraid to disappoint him. Some did not like him but everyone respected him. He did not tolerate shortcuts and could be hard to take if he felt you were not doing your best. I am a better person because I worked with him. Ultimately, Jim would stick to and stand up for what he believed, no matter what."

"Jim is a man of deep faith and strong will; his will is a God-given gift that was nurtured by his family as he grew up," explained Captain Ewert. "Jim has used this gift time and again to walk a pure path. Jim will work ten times harder and take the more challenging path versus the one of least resistance to reach what he believes is the right result."

Jim's convictions often led him to take an individual stance on issues important to him. "Jim's gray line is very thin," said Captain Ewert. "This is evident with his passions involving work, his dedication to his family, and a deep devotion to his religious beliefs and a desire to be right with his God."

As the new year broke, Jim seemed relieved that 2009 was over. During that year, a rattlesnake bit his grandson, who was hospitalized for days, his father had cancer that was successfully operated on, and his mother had a large tumor surgically removed. Each was treated in Sacramento at the University of California Davis Medical Center. When the new year arrived, all three were well, but Jim was not.

Jim repeated the Shema over and over as Scott, Nate, and God lifted him. Captain Ewert left Jim in the good hands of his teammates and headed out of the garage. Scott and Nate carried Jim from the inferno and laid him down on the grass. Nate pulled on Jim's gloves and the skin from his hands came off with them. They removed his jacket and stared at tissue that was essentially cooked to death. After removing Jim's pants, Nate reached under Jim's thighs and lifted him toward the gurney. He yelled to his fellow rescuers when he lost his grip and set Jim down again. The skin from Jim's legs peeled off as Nate tried to carry him to the ambulance.

"When I was in the fire I was taking account of my injuries," explained Jim. "As the burns progressed I could feel them spread. I could feel the depth of burn increase as well. I knew J.D. had gotten out when Nate reached me. Somehow he and Scott pulled me out of the fire and put me on the lawn."

Jim remained alert and conscious through all of this. "I remember that certain octaves of my screams made the pain a little more tolerable," Jim reflected. "I knew at the time that it was a very slim chance I would survive. In fact, I had come to the realization that my injuries were not survivable."

Jim called out for Captain Ewert and asked him to call his wife, believing he would not live to see her again. "Greg is a great firefighter and great friend, and it was only him I could trust with a final message to my wife. He was someone I trusted with my life, who my wife could trust and lean on."

J.D. ran over to Jim as he was pulled out of the house. "We both said, 'Are you okay?' at the same time and we each answered 'Yes.' I could see that Jim was not," recalled J.D. "His skin was like molten wax and it was just falling off. As I was loaded into my ambulance, the communication from Jim's ambulance sounded over the radio. I could hear the other medic calling in the report and heard Jim's screams in the background. I thought he was going to die."

To all on the scene, the collapse and rescue seemed like a lifetime, but these events unfolded in a relatively short period of time. Seven minutes elapsed from the time of the mayday call until Jim was pulled from the fire. Jim's memories of the event remain clear up until this point of the tragedy. "That last thing I recall was being loaded into the ambulance and driving away," said Jim. "My brother recently told me that my last words before being intubated were, 'That's it, I'm done.' I was drifting in and out at that point."

"As much as what went wrong in the instant the roof collapsed, after that everything went right," shared Greg. "Otherwise we would have had two or more dead firefighters." J.D. got out of the fire, the RIC crew was deployed quickly, and Jim and J.D. were instantly attended to at the hospital. "Every on-scene firefighter and medical personnel performed their job flawlessly," summarized Greg.

Jim first went to the local hospital, where doctors and staff stabilized him and facilitated his immediate transfer to a specialized burn center. It was too foggy to use a Life Flight helicopter so police cruisers escorted the speeding ambulance up the freeway as Jim fell unconscious from the trauma and the pain-killing drugs that coursed through his body. He arrived at the U.C. Davis Medical Center on a tightrope of survival.

J.D. suffered third degree burns on 10 percent of his body. He was initially hospitalized for a few days and then again for a week to treat infections to some of his burns. J.D.'s injuries were primarily to his buttocks and lower back.

Jim Adams suffered third degree burns on over 48 percent of his body. The fire burned the back of his head, back, buttocks, and thighs. Most of the skin burned off his arms as well and his left hand was almost completely destroyed. Pain from deep burns this extensive is incapacitating. Jim was kept in a medically induced coma, giving his body time to heal free of agony. In cases like Jim's, with this degree of damage, more patients die than live. Forced unconsciousness, multiple successful skin grafts, and the scientifically immeasurable will to live held Jim's only chances of survival.

Over the fifty-three days that Jim was in the hospital he endured many surgeries, countless infection-killing skin scrubbings, and many grafts simply to plug holes as he inched toward health. Jim was kept in a coma for three weeks. "Much of my coma time was spent in hallucinations including a recurring one with me trying to take the burden of asking Greg to call my wife," remembered Jim. "Asking him to reach out to her to tell her I was dying was a huge responsibility I put on him. In my dream state I kept trying to rearrange the position I put him in, to fix what I had done."

Jim does not know why he fell through the roof and why he lived. For a seeker of answers to thousands of questions in this enormous personal investigation, *why* remains a mystery. "It is simply too big to grasp," Jim shared. "I have wondered and wondered but cannot come up with an answer. For months after the accident I looked for reasons but could never truly understand it. So in this case I have stopped asking why."

He does, however, understand most of the *how* of his being alive. Within three hours of being pulled from the fire, Jim was at the U.C. Davis Medical Center's Firefighters Burn Institute Regional Burn Center, an intensive care facility designed specifically for injuries like Jim's. (See article page 39.) If the badly designed roof that collapsed was located in most other places around the country, Jim likely would have died. If he hadn't lived within ninety miles of one of the most talented groups of burn doctors and nurses on earth, his recovery would've looked far different. If he wasn't provided the best physiological and psychological care only those elite practitioners could give, his scars might have been too deep for recovery. "If he did not have such deep faith, the unflagging love and support of his family, and such a strong will he would have died," said Greg. "I know this, I think the doctors know this, and his community believes this. Others would not have survived these injuries."

"The doctors are some of the best in the world, and treated my injuries not only with great skill and compassion but also with the latest medical procedures," shared Jim, explaining how the state-of-the-art facility operates with an industry-leading holistic recovery approach. "The nurses are on the top of their game; they have an extensive knowledge base and an exceptional skill set, and they administer care with such compassion. Above all else, while I was in a coma and during my recovery they treated my wife and family with such tenderness and kindness that I will never be able to completely repay them."

"I was so afraid that I was going to lose him," recalled Amy. "He had always been a provider for our kids and me, doing everything for us. I did not know what I was going to do without him." The burn unit staff helped her understand the healing process. "They were not only Jim's doctors and nurses, but became like family and friends. They cared so much and took care of everything—big and small. They answered every question we asked and took the time to explain the process of what they were doing and the outcome they hoped to achieve. I was in pretty bad emotional shape and they seemed to know just how much news I could handle."

Firefighters also played a key support role. "Every single person in the department came in to see us. It was very emotional," recalled J.D. "Guys drove from Modesto every day to be with Jim and his family. Our department ran support like an incident response. Jim's and my family did not have to cook meals for a month. They mowed our lawns, did the laundry, and made sure there was always fuel in the gas tank. Just before the fire, I had stripped my entire house exterior to paint it in the days off I was supposed to have after the incident. As I lay in bed recovering, one day I heard a commotion outside. I stepped outside and saw thirty-five guys painting my house."

At the hospital, Modesto and Sacramento area firefighters who did not know Jim kept the media at bay, were at the ready to provide anything for his wife, and helped family and friends understand what Jim was enduring. "Two guys in uniform on revolving duty were always at the hospital, with credit cards in hand," continued J.D. "Oscar Barrera and Jeff Helvin, two firefighters who had recently survived bad fires, were especially important and kind in helping us deal with the emotional side of recovery. It was especially hard because we did not know if Jim was going to make it until they brought him out of the coma."

In the year following the accident, Jim endured four major skin graft surgeries and several reconstruction surgeries. The first were the most critical and life-saving. Doctors harvested healthy tissue from 35 percent of Jim's body. During the initial stages of his care over 83 percent of his body had damaged or compromised skin. Nearly every inch of his body either needed help or was needed to help him. His face, not badly burned because of his mask and the fact that he covered it with his left arm and hand, was the only part of his body left unchanged.

Jim's left hand, both arms and full backside suffered the greatest damage. His hand was so scorched that the bones were burned. It looked like a football-sized skinned puffer fish with boiled sausage-like fingers. Jim's buttocks and the back of his thighs were also destroyed. That permanently destroyed flesh had to be removed. Today, his arms are patchworks of skin taken from his lower legs and torso; skin that was meticulously applied to areas that had no skin of its own remaining. Jim's patchwork quilt of stapled skin grafts illustrates how delicately doctors must work when they have so little to work with.

Much of Jim's muscle was burned away or surgically removed. Scar tissue became like stiff straw on and in his skin. Physical strength was something he only dreamt about, and stamina was a bygone. But his conviction was not. He immediately began a physical therapy regimen, largely at home.

"When he first came back from the hospital we had to change bandages daily in order to clean tissue and redress it to help with the skin growth and prevent infection. This routine would take hours each morning," shared Amy. "Thankfully, I was able to take time off from work to help with that, but this vital routine continued for months even after I went back to work. I would also help with his physical and occupational therapy. There were many tear-filled days and nights, as the pain he was in and the work he had to do remained over-whelming."

"The therapy started very slowly, with simple things like learning how to sit up, stand, walk, feed himself and brush his teeth. Over time he got stronger, but only because he was determined to do so," said Amy. "Getting to the point where he could do more on his own and build up strength was a very long and painful process. He has always been a very proud and self-reliant man, so being dependent on someone else was not easy for him."

"He had a very tough road; every day of his early rehabilitation was absolute agony," recalled Greg. "The amount of pain he endured and pushed through was more than most people could take. So much credit goes to his wife and family who were by his side every day at the hospital and all along during his physical therapy. His faith and family made the difference."

Burn survivors face several recovery issues that are not readily apparent. These include nerve loss, itching, and range of motion problems as scar tissue becomes tight and stiff. "Part of my therapy became stretching the areas in my body that were severely burned," explained Jim. "My shoulders, wrists, elbows and the fingers on my left hand are tight, like being wrapped in cellophane. I constantly have to stretch these areas to maintain range of motion."

Skin is the most complex of all organs. With third degree burns, the nerves, sweat glands and hair are all lost. "Sensation on the majority of my body has been lost or altered," said Jim.

"I no longer place small items in my pockets because I can't feel them to retrieve them. Someone's touch is seldom felt, as well as sensing that I'm too close to the stove or other hot objects."

Burn survivors face other challenges not often thought of. "The loss of sweat glands produces some unusual sweat patterns, so I've had to learn new ways of monitoring my core temperature, and the itching is at times overwhelming," explained Jim. "This is caused by cells and tissues regenerating, the skin adhering to underlying tissue, and nerve changes and growth. After about a year and a half the itching slowed but it never stops and that is a challenge when half of your body itches."

Ten months after the accident Jim returned to partial duty work. While still recovering and undergoing multiple reconstructive surgeries, Jim assisted in the firehouses with non-emergency tasks. Just being able to walk, write, and drive were huge accomplishments. The media followed Jim's story from the night he was injured and gave significant coverage to his return. Jim was a hometown hero. While his colleagues kept the media at bay and the public relations officers of Modesto Fire Department served as a buffer, Jim accepted the media glare.

Jim recognizes that while he suffered significant loss, those around him also endured the emotional agony. He knows how others may be just an accident or a simple mistake away from his same challenges, and he dedicates himself to educating and supporting those whose lives are defined by fire.

"We all know, and now more than just intuitively, that life can change in a blink of an eye," reflected Greg. "We all learned a very valuable lesson. Before the accident Jim was a very private person. While he has always been very wise, thoughtful, and caring, now Jim has opened his life up to say thank you and to help others to try to prevent what happened to him from happening to them. He does this by teaching classes on fire safety, by publicly sharing his story, and through his incredible outlook on life."

Jim also rejoined the union. Firefighters who felt the sting when he left it still supported him and his family in the hospital. Jim repays this in myriad ways. He is now deeply involved with the Firefighters Burn Institute, attends national burn conferences, travels the state to give presentations, and visits equipment manufacturers to show the need for improved protection. (See article page 42.) He has turned his accident and scars into a gift for his colleagues by creating and offering classes on firefighter safety.

Jim realized an opportunity to help people through his experiences. "I never sought the limelight and still have trouble with it, but I feel an obligation to communicate what I have gone through in order to help protect firefighters, and for others to learn what burn survival means," said Jim. "The relationships I have developed through this process are very, very meaningful. Really, only other burn survivors understand the emotional and physical scars, and being able to share helps us all."

Jim and J.D. give presentations to firefighter agencies around the West. They emphasize the gear strengths and weaknesses, techniques that are imperative to saving lives, firefighter and victim medical care approaches, and protocols based on their experiences and recoveries. A typical presentation starts with an overview of the Modesto Fire Department, as detailed by Jim.

"We take a short look at the incident including time frames and response resources. J.D. then gives a powerful personal account of the incident and two months of our hospital stays. I give a personal account of my experiences," explained Jim. They present medical care and other issues experienced with rescue protocols, some of which they are changing within their department. "We also go into our personal protective equipment: how it works, limitations, etc., focusing mostly on the fact it worked and saved my life because I was wearing it. My point and focus is making firefighters aware of how susceptible we are to serious burn injuries and how to survive collapse and entrapment situations," said Jim.

Statistically, firefighters have one of the riskiest jobs in the world. I know this firsthand as members of my family are veteran firefighters who inspire me to pay homage to this community. My father-in-law, Ron Kovacs, fought fires for thirty-seven years with the Chicago Fire Department and is the patriarch of a clan of firemen. Two of his daughters are married to firemen and his son Ronnie Jr. is a firefighter too. Ron Sr. spent nearly four decades climbing ladders, axing through walls, crawling through smoke, jumping from ledges, falling through roofs, and operating fire hoses. These days he often talks with alumni firefighters and is always wearing his navy blue and white CFD sweatshirt.

Injuries and accidents among all firefighters take their toll. Ten years ago Ron was asked to leave the department because his heart was too overworked. He's familiar with many different recovery rooms from open heart surgery, a shattered elbow joint twice replaced, lungs racked from too much smoke, and a tricep muscle that still waits for reattachment. Perhaps his greatest pain of all is that his days and nights at the local firehouse are over. Now he plays a lot with his grand-kids, including my son and twin girls. He engages them in a game of runaway tickle and pulls them tightly into his arms. They don't know that one arm doesn't work too well. Love flows right through bad joints.

Ron remembers a time of solidarity when local firehouses pulled together to share personnel and equipment. "Fires in one part of town had made this a very busy area," he recalled. They did not have enough beds for everyone to stay at one sta-tion and drew straws to see who would go home for the night.

"The guys who drew the short straws and were supposed to go home would not leave," Ron continued. "We tried making hammock beds between the regular beds, but that did not work. So we drew straws again for beds versus chairs so that we all could go on the calls from the firehouse. Many of the guys just slept in chairs, and it lasted this way for a couple of weeks until the order to move back to the original firehouses came through."

This brotherhood lives on in the quiet of a firehouse lunch room where Jim and Nate sat down for an unplanned conver-sation nearly two years after the accident. Nate had not voiced his feelings with anyone except his wife and the counselor provided by the department immediately after the incident. Nate has replayed the incident many times in his head, won-dering if a better outcome was possible. The two men hugged.

"I wish I could have done more; I am so sorry for what you and your family have gone through," said Nate, eyes welling from years of bottled emotion. "I have never been able to talk about this and have felt guilty for so long about the emotional pain I have…when you are the one that got hurt." As tears fell, Nate continued. "I want you to know how sorry I am. I wish I could have done more." Jim whispered something to Nate and they hugged again.

A little over a year after almost dying, Jim returned to full active firefighter duty. He still pulls car accident victims from wreckage and works in burning buildings to extinguish fires. In spite of everything, he humbly considers himself "just a fireman." He explained the challenges that make him so much more:

> I became very focused on returning to work, which required getting stronger, getting to know my new capabilities, and relearning what I could handle physically and emotionally. Since I had lost so much skin and the nerves, I was unable to sense heat on a lot of my body as people with regular skin tissue do. I would put on my turnouts and go into the training facility with simulated fires in place. Over time we would increase the intensity of the training fires. At first I just wanted to make sure I could be in this situation psychologically. Then, it became a matter of understanding my new physical limitations. I had to get to know the heat of a fire in a new way. In essence, I had to figure out with new skin what was dangerously hot and what was not.

Jim cherishes suiting up and helping people as a firefighter. Above all, he cherishes those who brought him through the fire:

It has been a long road but I value every moment. My family and I are dedicated to live each and every day. I am unable to fully express my gratitude to those who helped me and my family get to this point. God has given me the strength not only to endure but to flourish. This community has been much of that strength. I believe the Shema means we are all one. There is unity among all things and every woman and man is the child of God. As I lay in the hospital with my entire life in question, my wife would read your letters and cards to me. My community never left me to fight this battle alone; they stood with me, following my story and me to this very day. I am so thankful.

"We have learned that life is short," reflected J.D. "I prefer now to spend more time with my family. I kiss my wife and hug my kids a little bit longer before I go to work. I know there is always a chance I won't be coming home."

U.C. DAVIS REGIONAL BURN CENTER AND BURN SURVIVORS

When Jim Adams was treated at U.C. Davis it was considered one of the best burn trauma centers in the country. Still it was not operating at the state-of-the-art level envisioned by its own medical staff. They dreamed, then built a newer facility that is now one of the premier burncare centers in the world. Robotics are used for ultra precise surgical procedures. Real-time global communications systems in operating rooms allow experts from around the world to consult with doctors on-site. Advanced therapeutic resources like infrared heat sources and hydrotherapy rooms enhance patient comfort and recovery.

The U.C. Davis Firefighters Burn Institute Unit is led by two of the leading burn surgeons in the country. Dr. David G. Greenhalgh and Dr. Tina Palmieri are experts in burn trauma and surgery. They have served as presidents or directors of national burn organizations and research associations, authored books on burn patient care, and now run one of the most highly regarded burn centers in the world. An information packet provided by U.C. Davis describes the center:

> The Regional Burn Center provides care to nearly three hundred burn patients from throughout the medical center's thirty-three-county Northern California service area. Patients are admitted for life-saving procedures, intricate wound assessment and management, as well as rehabilitation and psychosocial support and counseling. Two outpatient clinics provide services to patients who have less serious burn injuries.

Nearly two years after his accident, Jim and I walked into the unit. Jim hugged several staff members, took a step back, looked each one in the eye, smiled, and hugged them again.

Along with leading physicians, specialized medical tools and advanced procedures and research, compassionate care is equally responsible for rendering burn survivors instead of burn victims. Deb Jones, RN, and Len Sterling, RN, introduced themselves. Deb's specialty, in addition to physical patient care, is the emotional and mental recovery of burn survivors. Len is the manager of the unit and a practicing nurse as well. Deb spoke about her work:

> There are no burn victims. There are burn patients who become burn survivors. In order to assure this, we focus on holistic healing. Unique to burn patients are the scars that accompany their injury, and the societal stigmas that go along with that. We address this critical element to recovery as strongly and as soon as we deal with the physical treatment.
>
> The scars can be on the surface and deep inside. Our outreach program, which includes in- and outpatient counseling, outreach services such as newsletters and support groups, and social therapy retreats, addresses the need for patients and family to be comforted and guided through recovery. Recovery for us does not end when our client leaves the hospital. In most cases this is just one of the first steps.

U.C. Davis also serves as a teaching hospital, applying research and new technologies onsite. Some of these innovations saved Jim's life. Len and the doctors spend a significant portion of their time researching and creating new techniques. Len is an instructor for the American Burn Institute and has worked throughout the world offering treatment and pursuing new procedures to apply at Davis. New procedures are being developed now at an unprecedented rate, according to Len:

> Skin is our most complex organ. Consider all that it does: it contains nerves for touch and temperature sensation, has hair follicles and sweat pores for a variety of reasons, serves as our most important buffer to infection, and provides a thermal barrier for our body.
>
> When you step from a warm car to very cold air the stinging you feel is actually your skin contracting in order to thicken and protect your core from cold. When you are outside on a hot day you feel more flexible, which is your skin getting looser by getting thinner in order to let heat escape from your core. Trying to replicate skin is very tough due to its complexity.
>
> Unlike most organs, you

cannot transplant skin. We will temporarily graft skin that is not the patient's to temporarily help in recovery, but it will be rejected within two weeks. We do this in order to allow patients time to grow more of their own healthy skin that will then be cut from one portion of the body and grafted on to the burned portion. This requires multiple surgeries with considerable time in between.

Given this, recent research is focused on how to use the patient's own cells to grow more skin. Dr. Palmieri is involved in this research that is showing progress. Another technique that is seeing good results is the skin gun. This technique takes small pieces of skin down to the cell level. This tissue cell is then sprayed lightly on the burn area. This practice is being used overseas and we are involved in trial research in the U.S.

We have a very high level of expectations and quality at U.C. Davis and use a multidisciplinary approach to succeed in giving people the best possible quality of life after their accident. For example, our housekeeping and environmental staff hours as a ratio of payroll are among the top in the nation. The need to keep our unit as free of infection as possible mandates this. In addition, patients are kept in isolation during their time in the ward, for themselves and to reduce the possibility of cross contamination.

Another quality indicator is based on the general rule that a patient is hospitalized one day for every percent the body has been burned. U.C. Davis leads the nation in minimal time spent hospitalized using this ratio. This is a testament to our practices that focus on keeping infection rates low, using state-of-the-art therapies for improved healing, and helping our patients be best prepared physically and mentally for life after their hospitalization.

But, the real quality indicator is to look at a guy like Jim. We are so proud of what he has accomplished.

THE FIREFIGHTERS BURN INSTITUTE

In 1972 a jet crashed into a crowded ice cream parlor in Sacramento, California. Twenty-two people died in the crash and fire while scores more were badly burned. Local hospitals were overwhelmed by the demand for burn treatment and many patients did not receive adequate care. Based on this incident, then Fire Captain Cliff Haskell campaigned to improve burn care, education, and community services in Northern California. In 1973 he established the Firefighters Burn Institute. By his unwavering commitment over several decades, today the Institute is credited with the collaborative creation of the U.C. Davis Burn Unit and hugely successful community outreach programs for burn survivors.

Jim Adams' accident and the painful recovery process led him to The Firefighters Burn Institute. This offers recovery programs for burn survivors; provides fire and burn prevention information through public awareness campaigns; funds education for burn team professionals, firefighters, and burn survivors; and supports burn treatment and rehabilitation research. In the twenty-five years preceding the opening of the U.C. Davis Firefighter Burn Institute Regional Burn Center, the Institute raised millions of dollars to help fund the facility, while also raising awareness of the need for burn treatment.

Each year dozens of people survive and thrive as burn survivors, due in large part to Cliff Haskell's vision and dedication. In many ways, Jim owes his life to the Institute and today he serves as a powerful spokesperson for The Firefighters Burn Institute.

The Institute also sponsors adventure camps for young burn survivors. Each year, dozens of children from six to seventeen years old come from around the world to a wilderness setting filled with adventure, good cheer, and camaraderie. Here, children learn about themselves and others in a supportive setting that builds connections among recovering burn survivors. The ability to connect to others with similar emotional and physical challenges is a critical element in the recovery process. The camp glowingly facilitates this. There are also adult retreats and even a camp for very young burn survivors, from three to six years old.

When a firefighter is burned on the job and hospitalized at the U.C. Davis Burn Center, the Institute assists the family on a 24/7 basis by stationing a firefighter at the hospital. They do so to give the family a buffer from the media and to provide basic services of food, shelter, and transportation. This firefighter on standby provides the most emotional support and solidarity to the family. When Jim Adams was hospitalized, a rotation of firefighters served at his post for weeks.

The Firefighters Burn Institute is run and funded primarily by firefighters. The advisory board is composed of retired and working firemen and the executive director is a retired firefighter. Funds are collected primarily through firefighter "boot drives" and other donations.

Funding this organization is critical. Its work is invaluable. What started as the vision of one man transformed into a program run by experts who understand the impact of fires on individuals and their families. Their dedication to improved treatment and compassionate recovery is vital in the world of burn patients and survivors.

KELLEY KALAFATICH

Determination

The difference between the impossible and the possible
lies in a person's determination.
—TOMMY LASORDA

There have been times in my life that I wonder if I am
strong enough or brave enough to meet the challenge.
But with Kelley in the back of my mind in these situations,
I say "Yes I can" and overcome fear to succeed.

—TESSA SIBBETT

I n early summer of 1984, Kelley Kalafatich stood on the
bank of a wild river in the Sierra Nevada with wet suit, life
vest, helmet, and paddle, watching the current slam through
a narrow canyon. Tunnel Chute Rapid on the Middle Fork of
the American River churned into a wild maelstrom with the
melt of a deep snow pack high in the mountains. Slim, blonde,
and attractive, Kelley was a rarity; one of few female river
guides in an outdoor adventure industry dominated by men.

Six years earlier, when Kelley ran her first whitewater trip,
the idea of a woman guiding a raft full of paying clients down

a thundering river in a remote region of the world was met with skepticism. Still, she worked her way up through the ranks of the small, elite group of guides who traveled the world in search of evermore difficult rapids to run. She proved that maneuvering around life-threatening boils and through powerful hydraulic vortexes was as much a matter of cool-headed thinking and an instinctive understanding of the nature of fast-flowing water as it was physical strength or brute confrontation with the elements.

Kelley had a choice to make. She had to decide if Tunnel Chute was safe to run, or if her party would undertake the laborious task of portaging around the rapids. The International Scale of River Difficulty classifies the level of risk involved and the skills needed to navigate a river or single rapid safely. Placid, slow-moving water is rated Class I. Rivers rife with steep drops, violent currents, and a variety of other threats that raise the price of a mistake to injury or death are rated Class V. Rapids rated Class VI are considered impossible to raft. Tunnel Chute is a solid Class V.

The water below Kelley roared in a steep churning descent down a small canyon studded with jagged rocks. Only a week earlier a paying passenger was pulled from the bottom of the rapid with what his rescuers described as "God in his eyes" when a raft flipped in the violent current. Kelley studied the foaming cataract, running higher and stronger than she ever remembered.

I watched from the opposite bank. My clients and I launched a few miles upstream after Kelley began the trip with her group earlier that morning. I had never met Kelley but knew it was her—in those days most guides were male, heavyset, and not very pretty. Kelley's breach of rafting's gender barrier was already the subject of campfire conversations around the world. In an industry where macho mindsets prevailed, she was very determined to crack that ceiling. Determination, good judgment, focus, and a concern for the wellbeing of others are critical qualities in a guide's tumultuous trade.

I waited to see what Kelley would do. Was the steep stair-step drop a safe run, or too dangerous? Kelley watched the river a few minutes longer then signaled her waiting clients; it was too dangerous, the odds were too slim, and they would hike around. She jumped from rock to rock, jockeyed the rafts around the rapid, and got her guests ready to relaunch. I watched her move along the shore with the unmistakable glow of one deeply in love with a life of strenuous activity and rivers. I motioned to my clients to follow her lead on our shore. Kelley flashed a warm smile to us from across the river and paddled away with clients safely onboard, knowing even more adventure was just around the bend.

Whitewater rafting as an industry transitioned from infancy to adolescence in the late seventies and early eighties. Innocence shifted to bravado and risk taking. Several national and international rafting "first descents" were made on increasingly difficult rivers. Kelley was offered a job in Africa as a pioneering guide on the Zambezi River.

The Zambezi is Africa's fourth largest river. It forms the border of Zambia and Zimbabwe near Victoria Falls and is widely considered one of the wildest stretches of whitewater in the world. A voluminous cataract, the Zambezi flows at rates as high as three hundred thousand cubic feet per second, ten times that of the Grand Canyon's Colorado River.

In the mid-1980s Zambia—then one of the poorest countries on earth—was twenty years into independence and suffering, its economy dependent on price-crashing copper. Zimbabwe, freshly independent from British colonialism, was in better shape.

The town of Victoria Falls in Zimbabwe is perched on the canyon wall, a stone's throw from its namesake world wonder—the largest waterfall on earth. Tourists flocked to the "Vic Falls" Hotel for wicker high-backed chairs, five-course dinners, and down pillows. Livingstone, Zambia, the cross-the-border stepsister, was centerpieced with a windowless green-walled concrete disco hall blasting Bee Gees songs, and was rampant with labor strikes against the stifled economy.

Into this colorful picture walked Kelley and her fellow guides, employed by the leading international rafting company of its time: Sobek. Sobek was diversifying its worldwide whitewater adventure schedule. The Zambezi beckoned as a showcase destination and an economic driver for the region.

When the flooding river levels dropped after the annual monsoons, Kelley and her fellow guides sat at river's edge in the spray of Victoria Falls, known by natives as "Mosi-oa-Tunya" or "Smoke That Thunders." Although Sobek ran a few trips in prior years, this was the crew's first training trip. They studied the massive flow and yelled to one another above the rapid's deafening roar about river features more troubling than they had ever seen. Just to get to the launch point required hiking down a cliff on a two-foot-wide trail while shouldering rolled rafts. Local Zambians who knew the trails into the canyon helped as hired porters, but knew nothing about running the river. They were also given the chance to earn more money by learning a new trade with only one critical piece of equipment: a life jacket. Fearful of the river's roil, they nevertheless embraced their new jobs as "highsiders" and breadwinners in troubling financial times.

The four-boat flotilla—led by a guide who ran the river the year before—shoved off shore and into the expedition. Each raft dodged down the first rapid's best line but was tossed about like a cork in an ocean storm. Successive rapids lined up. Waves larger and less predictable than Hawaii's North Shore surf were plowed through and over. The boats dropped into huge, reversing, boat-eating holes—deep recirculating water on the downstream side of an obstruction that can cycle and recycle an overturned raft and its passengers until exhaustion and possibly drowning results.

The highsiders, quivering and bug-eyed, threw themselves as human ballasts to the high side of the raft that teetered on the brink of a cresting wave or crushing hole. One crew moved quickly enough to the airborne side of the boat and pushed it down with the mass inertia of their bodies. Another crew was a second too slow to leap across the raft and it tumbled over. The third raft's guide missed the narrow line to success through gigantic roller surf and flipped end-over-end. The river drew the fourth sideways into a hole but the highsiders' force kept it upright. As the group pulled ashore at the end of each subsequent training trip that week they saluted good fortune and knowledge gained.

Paying passengers began to arrive. The precious cargo of soaking wet guests who shared raft space with the highsiders now made good decisions by the guides more death-defying. Clients blithely deferred to their professional guides who, in spite of gained confidence and deeper experience with each monster rapid, wisely paid homage to the god of the river for safe passage. Kelley and the guides breathed relief and most clients were smiling at the end of each trip.

When the whitewater section of the river was too high to run safely, the guides led float trips through a mellow section of the Upper Zambezi. This section of river was as smooth as the Mississippi in paddle-wheel territory, with wildlife viewing as the ultimate reward. Leopards, giraffes, and elephants cruised along the shore as rafters drifted on waters with occasional crocodile and hippo sightings. As one trip led by Kelley and her colleague Mike Speaks neared the end, something unusual happened.

"I was about forty feet behind Kelley when this hippo sprang off the bottom, head-butted the bottom of Kelley's raft, and lifted it into the air," recalled Mike. "The hippo bit hard into the raft and all of the air on one side rushed out." Baffles inside the perimeter tubes of a raft hold air in several different chambers. When one portion of the boat deflates, the remainder of the raft will generally still hold air. "Even though some of the raft stayed inflated, people fell into the bottom of the boat from the hippo's force," said Mike. "The hippo took another bite and started tossing the raft around like a crazy dog with a rag doll in its mouth."

Two clients were instantly thrown legs skyward into the

air and landed in the water. The territorial hippo stopped biting into the raft and now prowled the waters around it. "Kelley kept her cool, reached into the river, and with one hand pulled one passenger and then the other back into the raft. She grabbed the oars and even though now half of the raft was flat, quickly rowed it to shore. We pulled it out of the water and saw that the hippo had ripped eighteen tears into the fabric," said Mike. The guides managed to repair the raft well enough to get back on the water and head to the finish point. "I was amazed at how Kelley handled all of this, which included getting back on the river," shared Mike. "We both rowed like crazy to get away from the hippo and to our take-out road."

When the river level dropped, the crew returned to the whitewater stretch below the falls. Locals who became more comfortable on the water were quickly promoted from porters to highsiders and then to training guides. These tribesmen—otherwise out of work ranchers, miners and farmers with an inborn respect of the river's power—sought gold in this new occupation. Here was a chance to put food on the family table.

They sat in the captain's seat—a plank of marine plywood bolted to a metal rowing frame strapped to the raft—oars in hands and eyes wide open. With Kelley and the professional guides they navigated whitewater madness, pulling or pushing at just the right time, cushioning off rocks that could pop the boat, and steering into the stabilizing path that kept them from tumbling over. Initially, successful runs were the exception and not the rule.

In a *Groundhog Day* cycle, Kelley and the trainees started

dry, flipped over, held their breath and swam to the surface, turned the raft back over, climbed back in, got dry, flipped over, held their breath, and swam to the surface. Over time, these dedicated young men became skilled river guides and gave the fruits of their labor to their families and community.

For four years Kelley guided and mentored on the Zambezi and traveled across the dark continent during her off seasons. Today the local economy prospers from guided trips on the Zambezi even as the national picture remains bleak. "Kelley was the most patient and loving of us all. She cared so much for the highsiders, who became cherished friends," shared Mike. "She quietly and humbly showed them how to get rafts safely down the river."

The new microeconomy financially saved local families and lives. "She knew the locals would be much, much better off if they could earn money that was coming in from outside their country. She dedicated herself to this cause," said Mike.

After Africa, Kelley traveled around the world to guide on more of the earth's most spectacular and challenging rivers. These included Chile's Bio-Bio, California's Upper Tuolumne, Siberia's Chuya River, and Alaska's Alsek and Tatshenshini Rivers. She also competed in numerous rafting world championships, winning several international competitions.

"Kelley was a huge cultural ambassador during these championships. Her kindness and gentleness won over people from all around the world," explained friend and fellow competitor Ronaldo Macedo. "She was always willing to help others and loved sharing stories and laughs with competitors and local villagers while she was winning race after race."

During this period, Kelley injured her knee and doggedly pursued her rehabilitation. "When she needed to rehab, her effort was off the charts," said Ronaldo. "She was my guest in Hawaii during this time, knowing that warm weather allowed her to train on her schedule."

Haleakala is one of the tallest mountains in Hawaii, with the road ending on the shoulder of the peak at ten thousand feet. Guided bike trips begin here, after tourists are shuttled up by van to cruise down the mountain. "Kelley's boyfriend and I would drive to Haleakala to paraglide down toward the beaches," shared Ronaldo. "Kelley would pedal up that road, which nobody does. She started at three thousand feet and climbed up, up, up to the ten-thousand-foot top. I had never seen that kind of determination, except for what she is doing today."

Once her knee healed, Kelley was recruited to run trips in her old river stomping grounds, the Sierra Nevada. As one of the world's most experienced guides she led river guide training schools, river conservation fundraisers, and all-women trips. Kelley joined and worked with a fledgling nonprofit organization: Friends of the River.

The group of friends and river enthusiasts lost their first battle to stop a dam from flooding the Stanislaus River, a free-flowing Sierra Nevada wilderness wonderland. Kelley supported the preservation of rivers as sanctuaries for people and nature alike while she organized and ran benefit raft trips. Her ambassadorship helped fund Friends of the River and she encouraged her clients to campaign against other dams. The organization's next effort—to save the Tuolumne River—was successful, as were many subsequent campaigns.

In these years, Kelley was the head guide on trips with dozens of training or junior guides. Many were young women hoping to become international river guides themselves. Sarah Lee Lawrence was one. "Meeting Kelley changed my life. I was taken with how powerful and caring she was. A lot of women in the river community can be just as exclusive as men. Kelley was not. She was open, empowering, and fun," remembered Sarah Lee. "She had run all of these international rivers and remained very humble and gentle. That is what is so impressive."

As with Sarah Lee, Kelley's impact on novice guides helped shape the adventure travel industry and each guide's future. "That summer changed my life. In very simple terms, people just love to be around Kelley. She is one of the most inspirational women on earth." Sarah Lee has logged over sixty thousand river miles on four continents, wrote a best-selling book and operates her own organic farm in Oregon.

"Kelley was so smooth and graceful as a river guide, but such a girl and so much fun in camp," remembered Tessa Sibbet, who trained with Kelley as an eighteen-year-old guide. They were on the Tuolumne River one frigid spring day, training for very high water runs with Class V rapids. The raft flipped and tossed Kelley and the trainees into the cranking ice-cold river. Kelley instantly climbed atop the upside down raft as others were sucked under and swept away. She threw a rescue rope to a nearby raft and barked at them to pull her closer to shore. As she did this, she pulled people up onto the raft with her.

"She showed no fear and never second-guessed what she was doing during that rescue," shared Tessa. "After running trips with Kelley there have been times in my life that I wonder inside if I am strong enough or brave enough to meet the challenge. But with Kelley in the back of my mind in these situations, I say 'Yes I can' and overcome fear to succeed. Kelley has never used being small or a woman as an excuse for anything. I list her as one of the top heroes of my life."

Meryl Streep also holds Kelley in high regard. During the 1993 filming of *The River Wild*, Kelley was cast as her stunt double. The whitewater in the film is real and its rapids are monstrous. During the filming on Montana's Kootenai River, Kelley was repeatedly asked to run twenty-foot waterfalls, dodge down boulder garden rapids and negotiate steep drops to capture the most spectacular footage. Through the numerous takes that increased the possibility of a catastrophic accident, Kelley kept her cool. The film won awards and no one involved was seriously injured.

Kelley's role in television and filmmaking expanded. She was featured in several adventure documentaries in locales from Borneo to Malawi. She participated in historic explorations and retraced Teddy Roosevelt's two-month trip through Brazilian wilderness on what is now called Rio Roosevelt. She followed John Muir's routes along coastal Alaska, chronicling his journey on a four-month backcountry adventure.

In 2001, Kelley coproduced, codirected and starred in a movie she filmed almost entirely herself. The movie, *Three Women, 300 Miles,* chronicles Kelley and her good friends Julie Munger and Rebecca Rusch swimming the entire length of the Colorado River through the Grand Canyon on river boards.

Grand Canyon river trips usually take place in the summer months when the icy cold water from the base of Glen Canyon Dam is a welcome relief from the triple-digit heat. The smallest vessels used on these trips are high-tech kayaks and sophisticated fourteen-foot-long rafts. Most boats are much bigger than that, including the monster thirty-two-foot-long pontoon rafts with outboard motors.

Overnight gear is strapped down in the rafts, forming a mini-mountain of ice chests laden with food and beverages, full-length cots, large camp tables, and cozy camp chairs. This mountain of gear climbs up and over eighteen-foot waves. Occasionally the river wins as rafts are flipped end-over-end, spilling gear and passengers into the cascading current. With the twofold benefits of this weight—raft stability and four-star outdoor accommodations—decadent wilderness comforts abound.

The three-woman river board expedition had no vestiges of luxury. Each swimmer carried all of her supplies on a second river board. This gear board was strapped around her waist with a quick release buckle and dragged behind her during calm sections. To maneuver, each swimmer had flippers that served as quasi-propellers. In the biggest rapids, each unstrapped her supplies board and held it next to her, except when huge waves ripped it from her grasp. Time and again, the women retrieved these boards in the calm below the whitewater storm and regrouped in moments of peace and quiet until the next big wave.

For nineteen days and nights, in the middle of winter, they swam some of the world's biggest rapids and pulled ashore each evening to meager rations and cold-weather camping. Kelley and coproducer Carr Clifton documented the entire voyage, what many consider one of the greatest wilderness stories of the twentieth century. Meryl Streep echoes this achievement as she ushers viewers into this award-winning movie with a moving introduction about the power of a wild river and the grace of its sojourners.

After the film, Kelley was among the first to raft Africa's elusive Blue Nile from its isolated and mysterious source. (See article page 73.) A first descent in arid Africa provided the perfect setting to make a documentary film illustrating the need to preserve natural places and free-flowing rivers. Kelley's nearly three-decade-long passion met her new-found love of filmmaking.

Rafting virgin rivers requires an entirely different set of rules. On regular commercial trips, no matter how difficult, the rapids are as familiar as the route to the corner store. You have a sense of what your crew should prepare for next. You know when the canyon is going to narrow, the waves escalate, and what that roar around the corner means. As with life, on first descents you wish you knew the river's game, but you don't. Such was the case for Kelley's last first descent.

The Blue Nile, one of the two originating tributaries for the mighty Nile River, is estimated by river-running experts as one of the most challenging on earth. Isolation, difficult rapids, territorial wildlife, warring xenophobic tribes, and various air and waterborne diseases converge treacherously. Kelley and the team of international river-running experts arrived in Ethiopia in July of 2004 to try their hand at navigating this backcountry. Their expedition followed centuries of similar attempts to overcome new frontiers as great as any on the planet.

The small group of adventure guides assembled with high hopes of running the river from source to sea. The trip's two visionary leaders, Les Jickling and Mark Tanner, were historians first and rafters last. They assured the veteran raft guides, Kelley, Scott Armstrong, and Sarah Lee Lawrence, that the equipment and logistics would be in place upon arrival. But at the small village rendezvous in Africa with expedition organizers, Kelley and her fellow raft guides and safety kayakers discovered expedition gear that was disheveled and incomplete.

Unease crept in among the guides. Kelley and her crew had a life-or-death decision to make even before shoving off into uncharted waters. The crew met away from Les and Mark to discuss options. They had traveled far to get to this point but were going deeper into the unknown with inappropriate gear and questionable leadership. The spirit of adventure prevailed, but under one condition: the experienced guides called the river-running shots.

At the headwaters of the Blue Nile, the crew left behind a week of significant gear preparation and days of grinding overland vehicle travel, biking, and hiking. The river sprang from Lake Tana and after a few lightweight river miles grew into the Northern Gorge Canyon. Quiet waters shifted into screaming torrent constricted by Grand Canyon-style walls, elevator steep drops, and sharp blind corners. Each day the crew followed a similar routine: the kayakers paddled ahead and ran unknown rapids, pulled into pocket-sized shoreline eddy calms and signaled the raft guides to run a fine line path they found suitable.

Crests of waves smashed down onto the rafters, boulders instantly appeared from the muddied waters, and crags in the rocky walls secured the guides' desperate reaches to stall the rafts in calms above new cavalcades of whitewater. At times the river ran impossibly hard. Class VI rapids signaled first as a roar and then a horizon line across the river. Sections were impassable due to deadly sieves and locomotive-sized holes. Here, the crew pulled ashore, untied all the gear, and shouldered it along precarious ledges around the fluid death. After a week of hard-won luck and skill-based successes they emerged from the gorge.

As the whitewater softened, other dangers intensified. Disturbed hippos and hungry crocodiles patrolled the river around every bend. Extreme changes in water levels made it difficult to predict what each day would bring. Riverside beaches for camping and safe anchor for the boats were scarce and illnesses known only to this part of the world made some sick.

Ten days of extreme river travel later, the team sensed the nearness of their take-out point just inside the Ethiopia-Sudan border. The river grew in size but mellowed, and now Les and Mark paddled folding kayaks that were carried on the rafts. They separated from the rafters, running smaller braids distant from the main channels. The rafters searched for the road to take them out of the canyon, one which Les and Mark planned for. They pulled ashore just downstream of a creek where a cable stretched across the river, with no road in sight.

They were met not by a welcome party but by villagers and soldiers who questioned their arrival. These Sudanese military troops were not happy with this unannounced invasion, but through sign language and broken English the team convinced the Sudanese that they were not a threat. Les and Mark arrived by kayak to an unceremonious welcome by their crew. There was no promised road out and they were in Sudan—a country in the midst of violent conflict—not Ethiopia.

The guides dismantled the rafts and moved the gear upriver, with the Sudanese soldiers graciously carrying load after load. They bade Les and Mark farewell on their journey to kayak the Nile to the ocean, feeling their time adventuring together was more than sufficient. One hundred and twenty days later, Les and Mark reached the Mediterranean as the first self-powered expedition to travel the Nile from source to sea.

For three days the guides toiled to get their gear from the river to the closest town, Bambza, where they staged for the arrival of their equipment truck. It never showed. Each night locals fed and bedded down the exhausted, mushy-legged crew. On the fourth day their truck driver rode in on bike with news that his truck was stuck in the mud one hundred miles away. Locals supplied pack animals to carry the gear fifteen miles past washed out bridges while guides and livestock owners alike carried more gear by hand.

The guides parted from their adoptive caregivers with a borrowed truck that groaned for hours along the way to their equipment rig, which was pulled out of the mud by tribesmen who anticipated their arrival. "The local people were so wonderful, loving and always greeting us with huge smiles…

even though they are so poor, you couldn't imagine," recalled Kelley. "We were always made to feel welcome. Without their help, we'd probably still be there!"

Two days later the team reached Addis Ababa, the capital city. They boarded modern transport for the first time in weeks and lifted off for home. While the team toasted to survival and the heart of adventure, Kelley was unaware that life change had wormed its way into her blood stream without permission.

Three years after running the Blue Nile and within a forty-eight-hour period, Kelley lost strength and sensation in her legs. This was immediately followed by back pain that progressed from mild to excruciating. The problems escalated to total numbness in her upper legs, inability to urinate, and extreme sciatic nerve pain. Kelley admitted herself into the hospital as symptoms worsened. She lay in the hospital for days as physicians struggled to determine the cause of the paralysis and excruciating nerve pain.

A large cyst on an ovary was first diagnosed as the problem since it appeared to press against her spinal cord. The cyst was removed but the pain and nerve loss intensified. Subsequent scans revealed numerous lesions on her spinal cord in a manner unfamiliar to American doctors who could not determine their cause. Kelley continued to spiral downward, her pain essentially intolerable. Those who have suffered from a pinched nerve may comprehend to some degree the pain that even deeper nerve trauma would bring. Lesions on the protective sheath around the spinal cord are infinitely more painful than nerve compression.

The following excerpt from Kelley's November 2, 2007 blog entry written by her friend Julie Munger described that red-hot pain, and frustration of the initial hospital days:

> KK is still trying to get the pain drugs under control. She is resting and her team of pain doctors is trying to find the right combination of meds to keep her awake and alert and out of pain! Progress toward this goal is good and it takes time to get the drugs in her system and see how she reacts.
>
> They are doing another spinal tap later today. They are still trying to identify the specific antigen that is causing the lesion/inflammation on her spinal cord. At this point, the lesion is in the lower lumbar spine and she is still paralyzed from the waist down. The prognosis is still unknown. She may get better; she may not.

Doctors were unable to diagnose what infected her. Early in her hospital stay, Kelley asked the doctors to check for schistosomiasis, a waterborne parasite that Africans often contract and die from. As it was such a rare cause of concern in America, they continued to look elsewhere for the problem. They considered lupus and multiple sclerosis, but could not explain why the strange lesions riddled her spine. Blood tests ruled out more common neuromuscular disorders.

Spurred by Kelley's repeated requests to check for schisto, they finally did—almost four weeks after she entered the hospital. The test came back positive. A tangible and actionable diagnosis was a relief and provided some hope, yet the delay in discovering the root cause of her nerve pain and paralysis gave the infection time to take a deeper hold. The nerve damage to her spinal cord was catastrophic.

Schistosomiasis or bilharziosis is a microscopic waterborne, flatworm parasite found primarily in tropical Africa. Most commonly, schisto enters its victims through the skin, transferring to the lungs via capillaries where it mutates before settling in the liver. Once in the liver the parasite can cause severe gastrointestinal problems and even death. If diagnosed early, the prescribed drug treatment kills the parasite and the victim returns to health. However, an atypical path of schisto can render great complications.

Generally, fewer than 10 percent of those infected by schisto experience central nervous system problems. But in rare instances, the eggs of the flatworms migrate to the brain or spinal cord and create lesions that seriously compromise or destroy neurological functions. Time is of the essence when this occurs.

According to internal medicine experts Shaji Habeebulla, MD, and John J. Ross, MD, "Spinal cord schistosomiasis is an infectious disease emergency. Outcomes in spinal cord schistosomiasis are worse with delayed diagnosis and treatment. Only 19 percent of patients make a full recovery. Rates of full or partial recovery are lowest for patients with transverse myelitis," a debilitating outcome of spinal schistosomiasis. Transverse myelitis is a fancy way of saying localized spinal cord destruction.

Rehabilitation became a way of life for Kelley, but the

piercing nerve pain from the lesions exacted a price for the work needed to regenerate those very nerves. Workouts designed to rebuild nerve and muscle to walk caused lightning-sharp nerve pains to course through her back and legs. Physical therapy, pain pills, fundraisers, donations, and visits from friends now defined Kelley's days. A blog entry from a few years ago after a fundraising event expressed Kelley's gratitude:

> My dear friends and family, I thank you from the bottom of my heart for your support in coming to the benefit…I was truly overwhelmed and was so happy to have gotten the chance to say hello to so many! And I am sorry for the ones I didn't. I was sitting, relaxing in the sun over the weekend, recovering and reflecting on our Friday night, trying to remember all the folks I spoke with or just saw from a distance hoping to say hi. Remembering off the top of my head…all of you wonderful people who are part of my life…
>
> It has been two years since I have been paralyzed and not a day goes by when I have not thought about how deeply grateful I am to the people who have contributed to helping me physically, spiritually, and financially. I continue to get better every day, and every day there is a new light of hope. To you all, thanks for helping me to be strong. I love you guys.

Kelley's next two years were a series of metaphoric steps forward and back. She lived with friends and family who built a physical and emotional safe haven to ease the tribulations of life in a wheelchair. In the midst of all this, Kelley suffered another blow from a bad fall taken in her front yard. The wheel of her chair caught a hole she didn't see. "When I hit the hole I fought to stay in my seat and I couldn't reach the ground with my hand because of the slope," recalled Kelley. She fell hard. "I landed hard on my knees and my butt then slammed back on my calves. I pried the distal femur off like a bottle top. Both of my femurs were badly broken."

In 2010, after months recovering from this accident and recognizing the need for targeted therapy, Kelley moved to San Diego County and now lives there most of the time. She moved away from her support network to be close to Project Walk, an organization dedicated to improving the lives of people with spinal cord injuries through exercise, education, support, and encouragement. (See article page 75.)

Kelley lives in an apartment with Wilbur, her trusty side-kick dog and her mom, retired from decades as an elementary school teacher in Montana. (See article page 77.) "The thing at the top of my to-do list is to walk, and it takes up every minute of my time. It has been pretty crazy trying to deal with this," explained Kelley. "It scares me to think about being paralyzed, not being able to walk, and in pain for the rest of my life," she continued, shifting from one hip to the other in her wheel-chair. "I miss being outside. I miss being on the river."

Project Walk is a bright place. The Southern California sun beams in through big windows, motivational quotes with foot-high letters adorn spring-colored walls, and high-fives and pats on the back abound. Ambulatory visitors *walk* in as their loved ones—patients with steely fight—put one foot slowly in front of the other. Among those who don't use a wheelchair and are not in pain, "problems" shrink to insignificance.

At Project Walk, Kelley straps herself into a metal frame and stands straight up after smiles and traded encouragement. The much needed pressure on her hips and legs helps to stimulate bone density growth. She remains upright for ten minutes with eyes closed as nerve pain grows and shifts in this position. She occasionally peeks around, shifts grimace to slight smile, and politely implores her new friends to keep working as they implore her.

Kelley then joins her therapist on a workout table about the size of a queen bed. She grabs the exercise pad beneath her as she would oars in the biggest rapids. Her grasp anchors her as she lifts her legs in the air—willing them to move. For now just her hips and upper legs obey the command. For an hour, veins in her forehead bulge, her cheeks redden, and sweat pours off her face.

Muscles, nerves, and raw emotion fire powerfully on all cylinders. She moves to the edge of the table and sits upright, legs dangling in the air. Together, Kelley and her therapist grunt and silently beg nerves to speak to withered muscle and move her feet. Her mind forges new neural networks, allowing motor neuron signals to trigger synapses necessary for movement. Essentially, Kelley's will to walk makes tiny movements in her ankles and feet. Medical terms aside, nothing is left on the rehab table.

Next is the stationary bike. Kelley pedals, the front tire

moves, and progress is marked. What was not possible just a few months ago—a single revolution of the bike wheel—is now twenty minutes of feet and tire rotating. After the bike, Kelley tries to leg-press her own body weight on the slant board for fifteen minutes, using muscles that are slowly but surely reigniting and strengthening. Purpose and pain saturate this workstation.

Over two hours and pints of sweat later, Kelley transfers to the electric nerve stimulation stationary bike. This piece of equipment assists riders with pedaling motion while firing nerves through electric impulses. Kelley's muscles are fatigued at this point so the equipment takes over. She closes her eyes and imagines getting up out of a chair and walking without piercing pain, breathing deeply and taking her mind to better places.

Three hours after arriving, Kelley unhooks herself from the bike, eases back into her chair and rolls toward the exit, hearing in the distance her trainer's reports of gain. The day-to-day changes are small but measurable and viewed over months, the improvement is awe-inspiring. Kelley passes her cohorts—the teenager who proudly tosses a tennis ball a few feet in the air and the young father who sobs with joy at each halting step—bidding everyone farewell with a soft touch of encouragement. At her van, she powers herself onto the wheelchair lift, transfers to the driver's seat, grabs the throttle and heads home. There she climbs into bed utterly exhausted.

"Kelley is the most powerful woman I have ever met in the most natural, gentle, and graceful way," explained Sarah Lee Lawrence. "An inner core of capability and strength define her. She taught me so much about myself, the river, and love.

Of all the people I know, she is the one that can overcome this. She will walk again."

Mike Speaks expressed similar admiration for Kelley's ironclad strength:

> From dropping into the massive jaws of the rapids of the Zambezi River (the first woman to kayak it), to riding a boogie board down the Grand Canyon, to repeatedly doing wild stunts as Meryl Streep's double in *The River Wild*, to facing off charging silverback gorillas in Zaire, to winning numerous whitewater competitions, to throwing back vodka with Russian rafters in the Altai Mountains of Siberia, to more recently trying to learn to walk again, Kelley Kalafa-tich has never flinched.
>
> She has helped thousands live their dreams by guiding them through adventure and wilderness. Her life choices have taken her to all corners of the globe in pursuit of adrenaline and the camaraderie found among like-minded people. If most of us had a fraction of the courage she has, the world would be a much better place for us all.

In a series of recent blog posts Kelley wrote from her summer home at her mom's place in Montana, she revealed both triumph and struggle on her journey toward walking:

> Since mom and I arrived in Montana, a month has passed to the date. I've been in so much nerve pain.

It has been quite cold. Ro [Kelley's physical therapist in Montana] has been working with me…. the combo of work and cold, the nerve pain has been terrible! I have not been comfortable in so long. Ro and I have decided to slow down with rehab and rest more; hopefully I'll start to feel a little better. It is so, so unbearable most of the time. I am so sad and depressed. Onward! I gotta keep going and not give up.

It has been so long, I forget what it feels like to not have pain. It has been so long since I've been on a river. I miss my river buddies. I miss Alaska, and the quiet beauty of the northern rivers and all the adventure.

I've been wanting to write on the blog but I kept getting blocked by either rehab, resting, or dealing with nerve pain…it's been difficult for me. Not only for the pain but in not wanting to talk about it; either on paper, computer, or telephone. I just find it depressing, and when I communicate with friends and family I want it to be positive.

Lastly, for my two angels Mom and Ro who have been taking care of me and cheering me on every day, I am eternally grateful. Mom has been with me every step of the way…helping me with everything imaginable…without her I don't know what I would do.

And for Ro, I'm so fortunate to have Ro Fundum… she is so committed to me and very knowledgeable. She's worked as a personal trainer for several years and during that time, for three years, she competed in bodybuilding. Now tell me how lucky I am! Ro's incorporated her bodybuilding skills toward building nerves!

Meryl Streep, among the others, expressed much praise for Kelley and her undying spirit of positivity and adventure:

I knew Kelley in the days when she was famous as a river rafter and kayaker, for her undaunted certainty in her body's ability to tackle the toughest course. Her glory in her physical being, her athletic bravery, her personal grace—all of these things had to morph into a different shape after the illness that shook her world; when she had to reconceive that world, and how to navigate it. Kelley's story is one that anyone can take to heart, no matter what your particular challenge. The inspiring and honest telling of how she managed to come to a deeper, fuller appreciation of the gift of living is one of the good news stories that resonate within every life.

In her few decades on earth, Kelley has experienced several lifetimes of adventure and camaraderie and one long, unwelcome challenge delivered by the strange hand of fate. She has helped to create a generation of people who live their dreams. Now she is working to rebuild her own.

Kelley's reach today extends beyond the shores of a wild river as she shares stories of passion and persistence from auditorium stages. Rapt audiences learn lessons of true determination from her. From river guide to stuntwoman and filmmaker, she is now a person yearning to walk and live pain-free. As an inspirational speaker, she has earned the right to illuminate for all of us the gift of courage. She tells us how to embrace challenge, live our dreams, and give our unique gifts to the world, which makes us all better.

NILE RIVER HISTORY, DAMS, AND FREE FLOWING RIVERS

The history of the Nile River is rich and tragic. Time and hearsay have attempted to romanticize the scenery, solitude, and sorcery of the river, but the true risks of its exploration were never eclipsed. Even today those traveling its course face dangers that have long existed. Early explorers who made it into the headwater territories consisted primarily of missionaries and merchants who were repelled by man, beast, and disease. The colonization of Africa in the 1700s and 1800s amplified the quest to find the wellspring of the longest river in the world, but "The Great Prize" remained elusive as explorer after explorer returned unsuccessful. Most believed that Lake Victoria, feeding the White Nile, was the primary source of the river. Presumably Dr. Livingstone found this feeder in the 1860s. Early 1900s expeditions located Lake Tana in the Ethiopian Highlands and discovered that it was responsible for the vast majority of the river's flow.

For more than nine thousand years the Nile flowed unfettered from the headwaters to the sea, serving the civilizations along its route. At over three thousand miles long, it drains millions of acres in an annual flood and drought cycle unmatched by any on earth. This variation in flow caused problems for civilizations engaged in agriculture and animal husbandry, which led to the perceived need to harness the life-giving and life-damaging power of the river.

The first dam was built in 2900 BC to protect lower river communities from radical annual high and low flows. For centuries thereafter, small dams were built to enhance farming practices and protect towns. The river valley became heavily populated because of its fertile alluvial grounds. Pressure for more protection from floods, electrical power demands, and essential water supplies led to the 1971 construction of the Aswan Dam in Egypt. Lake Nasser then flooded a huge portion of the Nile Valley behind the Aswan. Subsequent dams were planned and built upriver in Sudan and Ethiopia. Populations grew exponentially in the area as the harnessed river allowed for greater development. This rapid growth and the plans for more dams prompted Kelley and her team to attempt to raft from the Nile's source to the sea—a feat to recognize the world's greatest river and the folly of unwise dams.

Kelley Kalafatich and other river enthusiasts have long supported the need for free-flowing rivers and have fought against the building of dams for decades. Several organizations including Friends of the River, American Rivers, and The Nature Conservancy have pioneered this process, seeking the demolition of dams that were unwisely built during construction-heavy years when government money flowed freely. In those years dams were seen as necessary for flood control, power production, lake recreation, and job security. Now dams are being removed to return rivers to their natural state, honoring the value of productive fisheries, the recreational benefits of peaceful waterways, and respect for natural cycles and the health of the planet.

Most nonprofits dedicated to wilderness protection understand the need to balance population growth with the conservation and preservation of wild places. In recent years their efforts and those of local residents and various government officials have led to the removal of The Great Works Dam on the Penobscot River in Maine, the Conduit Dam on Washington's White Salmon River, the Simkins and Union Dams on the Pataspsco River in Maryland, and hundreds more. In addition, four dams on the Klamath River in Oregon and California, one of the longest rivers in America, were listed by the federal government for removal in the next few years. Nearly one thousand dams of consequence have been removed in the U.S. in the last hundred years, the majority of those in the past two decades. The dedication of Kelley and other river lovers to the protection and restoration of waterways is paying off. Though vital in some cases, dams can be a waste of natural processes and beauty. Exercising discernment in how they are used is leaving America with more free-flowing rivers than before.

PROJECT WALK

When I walked into Project Walk for the very first time, I felt energy that was at once electrifying and subduing. The passion, drive, and determination to simply move a leg, an arm, or a finger was overpowering. In spite of the tragedies that brought people there, its atmosphere radiated hope. In ten minutes' time, I was astounded by the courage of a community striving to heal and overcome.

In the Project Walk rehabilitation center, spinal cord injury patients are resolute to take one step or raise an arm. Trainers, family members, friends, and others gather around loved ones who force themselves to move an inch or a foot.

The power of will in this specialized gym is unmatched. Determination and hardworking individuals define the environment. Time and again I said to myself that this organization should never have a funding issue. Anyone and everyone who can benefit from Project Walk should have access to it.

Ted and Tammy Dardzinski, previous owners of an athletic performance center, and Eric Harness, an exercise kinesiologist, founded Project Walk in 1999. Today it is universally regarded as the pioneer in exercise-based recovery for spinal cord injuries. People from around the world seek help at Project Walk. On any given day folks from California, India, Ireland, Norway, and Brazil are at work there to improve their lives.

For the more than one thousand people who have come, Project Walk is a blessing. Countless client stories of conventional medical treatments and previous facilities that failed to provide meaningful hope or therapy testify to the power of this place.

Many clients describe therapy at traditional facilities as providing guidance for life in a wheelchair and little more. Project Walk is different; therapists realistically face patients' debilitating injuries by providing guidance and systems to overcome them.

According to recent research gathered by Eric Harness, 71 percent of Project Walk patients gained use of motor function from nerves that were damaged below their level of injury. In layman's terms, if significant nerve damage is suffered in the upper cervical spine, the body is immobilized below that location. Function below the injury indicates nerves are sending signals to muscles by working around the actual location of the injury.

In cases observed at Project Walk, sensation and at times mobility below the injury level is possible. Clients with a spinal cord injury, who historically would have no function of their legs because of the injury location, experienced significant improvement with Project Walk protocol. Many were told by traditional practitioners not to expect any muscle performance or to walk again.

Despite overwhelming evidence of success, insurance companies do not typically cover treatment at Project Walk. For most clients the travel, assessment, personalized exercise routine, and ongoing participation in the program are out of financial reach. This is the case even as Project Walk charges approximately 30 percent of what more traditional physical therapy programs ask.

On the wall in huge letters at Project Walk is the mission statement: "Using Exercise to Move Science." Project Walk's proactive approach to stimulate nerve and muscle growth through exercise is gaining recognition among physicians and hospitals.

The success of nerve therapy continues to grow and appear in new research. Project Walk's success is measured in greater value by those who did not walk in, but in weeks or months or years of hard work and ceaseless faith, did walk out. As brilliantly stated by Eric Harness:

"Project Walk gives hope to people who were told to have none."

GUIDING THROUGH RELATIONSHIPS

Being an international river guide has tons of rewards and just a few liabilities. With the benefits come rare but real risks of injury, as Kelley knows. Another potential downside is the lack of opportunity to develop a meaningful relationship with someone special. Deep emotional attachment to a life partner is challenging when your preferred line of work involves leaving for days, weeks, or months to faraway places.

Clients are companions for limited periods of time. They come on outfitted wilderness river expeditions because they want and need the expertise of experienced guides. Guides fulfill most of the guests' hierarchy of needs including food, shelter, and emotional support as guests live largely outside their comfort zone.

Ironically, many river guides never marry or find a partner with whom to grow old. Others do later in life, with decades of guiding and sharing the beauty of wilderness behind them. Cherished friendships among fellow guides are bonds created by risk; not many jobs require you to wear a *life* jacket to work every day.

Kelley has been deeply in love and knows the challenges and joys of long-term relationships, but today does not have a partner. After living a river guide's life for nearly three decades and constantly giving to others, learning to accept absolute deep love and receive genuine care requires a shift in her existence. With a legion of friends and supporters, Kelley is making that shift.

JOSH KERN and THURGOOD MARSHALL ACADEMY

Confidence

When we let our own light shine, we unconsciously give other people permission to do the same. As we are liberated from our own fear, our presence automatically liberates others.

—MARIANNE WILLIAMSON,
used by Nelson Mandela in 1994 inaugural speech

At some point you reach a fulcrum where what lies ahead is easier to accomplish than anything you faced in your past. With anything I now face, I believe I can achieve.

—JAMES WATKINS, Thurgood Marshall Academy graduate

On a typical weekday morning, the Washington D.C. metro commute from affluent Virginia to the south end of the nation's capital is packed with a sea of swaying white-collar professionals. Silently, with no eye contact, they begin their day on a fast-moving train. Thousands of riders, most with their dreams left at home, head into the political heart of America. Underneath downtown D.C., people pour out of the underground train and up into daylight via escalators to the streets of policy and promise. Those who stay on for two more stops or happen to get on at this station are different. Their numbers are few. By the time the train reaches Anacostia station, in a neighborhood of projects located in Ward Eight of our nation's capital, the remaining few dozen riders filter out wearing fashions of the hood.

The neighborhood around Anacostia station is composed of run-down homes, overgrown vacant lots, shuttered businesses, and an elementary school with a lineman-sized security guard at the front door. A few people walk to work—or not. Gangs post up on corners and people wishing they were somewhere else roam the streets. There are some signs of hope—an Open sign blinks in a deli and friends paint an elderly neighbor's fence—but all is far from well.

Ward Eight has the greatest percentage of ex-cons and poor people in D.C. Over one-third of the population lives below the poverty line. In February 2011, it had the highest unemployment rate in the country, with a full 25 percent of its population trying to survive without jobs. In 2010, there were over two thousand eight hundred violent crimes reported in the area. The bleak environment behind these statistics makes the education of its children virtually impossible at worst and daunting at best. But on the corner, opposite the metro station, sits a beacon of opportunity.

Across from the metro station, Thurgood Marshall Academy welcomes students like Darrion Willis. "I lived on the other side of Ward Eight and had to take the bus or the metro to get to school. For years, I would get hassled by a group of guys who stood at the entrance of the metro, blocking it with a human barricade," remembered Darrion. "You could not get around them. They would ask me questions and force me to look at them and talk to them, knowing that I was not from this area and was going to Thurgood Marshall. They wanted to intimidate me."

With time on their hands and turf to protect, gangs prowled the neighborhood. "It was their hobby to beat people up. I always tried to ignore them but they would not leave me alone," Darrion continued. They jumped him. "It was very scary and I had to get away by running across the street to the school. I had to watch my back every single day."

At the entrance of Thurgood Marshall Academy is a concrete staircase and an intercom button on the porch to reach the school's front office. The stoop is noisy and fully exposed to the street and metro station entrance. Guests stand there warily looking around and waiting for the door to buzz and unlock for passage. With a friendly but guarded "May I help you?" the secretary at the front desk greets visitors. After verifying they belong there, she warmly ushers them into the school.

With the first step inside fear melts away, replaced by clean, shiny marble and wood. High school kids tease one another and a kind secretary maintains a watchful presence. The stately historic building—a former public school now upgraded with state-of-the-art educational technologies—is an academic and community haven. Outside there is desperation and dashed hopes. Inside lies order, kindness, desire, and dreams coming to life.

When I visited Thurgood Marshall Academy, I experienced trouble trying to get to the school. The bellhop in front of my comfortable confines at the Hilton Hotel, in D.C.'s Embassy Row, hailed a taxi for my trip to Ward Eight. I got in the back seat and shared my destination with the driver. He told me he could not take me there. Thinking that he had limited time to make this cross-town run, I climbed out and the bellhop hailed another taxi.

Again, the driver told me "no can do." After growing frustration and disbelief, the fourth taxi driver agreed to take me to Anacostia. He told me how the crime and poverty numbers stop most people from going there to work, to visit, or to live. He said that Anacostia was a dangerous place and he too was very uncomfortable there. Nevertheless, we made the trip. I paid my fare, thanked the aberrant driver and climbed the steps to the front door.

Amid the violence and despair that for decades riddled Anacostia, in 1999 a young law student was asked to teach public high school kids as part of his law degree coursework. That student, Joshua Kern, grew up in a small Pennsylvania town of fifty thousand people as the son of an educator who instilled in him the value of being a teacher. Josh's hometown is described on the community website:

> The Township of Lower Merion [the "Township"], first settled in 1682 and well known as an attractive and affluent residential community, is located along Philadelphia's famed Main Line in "Delaware Valley, U.S.A." Fine homes and estates, excellent highways, exclusive shops and department stores, luxurious apartment houses, stately church edifices, some

buildings dating back to the 17th century, and superior public, private and parochial schools and colleges characterize the Township. Lower Merion Township remains Montgomery County's most affluent and populated municipality with the highest incomes, largest labor force, highest ratio of white collar and professional workers, most households, most single-family detached dwellings, and most married residents.

Lower Merion has the fifth highest per capita income in the country. Its population is 86 percent Caucasian. White-collar employees constitute 87 percent of its workforce. Less than 2 percent of its families live below the poverty line. An idyllic upbringing in places like the Township is one that thousands share: small town comforts, no money worries, and neighborhood security. Mighty few from this Norman Rockwell environment grow up with a burning desire to work in neighborhoods of turmoil and violence.

In a class aptly named Street Law, Josh Kern and his fellow law students were required to teach teenagers about the legal system. Josh's placement was at Ballou High in Ward Eight. Low expectations and high-alert security systems formed a reputation at Ballou. Metal detectors and dusty textbooks defined the school.

Teachers who lacked resources and dumbed down curriculum for students perplexed Josh. Goals, objectives, desires, and tools to teach students effectively were scarce. Teenagers who graduated generally did so unprepared to succeed in the community or in college. Most were more concerned with surviving than thriving.

A few short years after he graduated from a safe Jewish high school, Josh and college classmate Lee McGoldrick stood in front of their Street Law professor pleading for the opportunity to create a program for at-risk, inner-city D.C. kids. Josh could not ignore his need to help these students. He wanted to create a college preparatory school in an underprivileged area of the city. "Why," he wondered aloud to anyone who would listen, "should kids who want that have to go all the way across the city?" The professor agreed to the proposal provided they complete the program syllabus by the end of the semester. They had two months to create a curriculum that would enable opportunities for kids in this dysfunctional public education system.

Josh and Lee brainstormed night and day to figure out how to reach these kids in a meaningful way. They felt a few key ingredients to a child's growth were missing from the present system: love, structure, security, and promise. They built on these fundamentals and created on paper a charter school that they intended to open in Anacostia. With their professor's approval and the approval of the Washington D.C. Charter School Board, Josh and Lee's plan became a reality.

Josh secured space for the impending Thurgood Marshall Academy in an often-flooded church basement. With the help of other law school students he tried to attract students. In a series of misguided meetings and neighborhood campaigns to garner interest, doors were literally and metaphorically slammed in his face. White people from the other side of town telling a largely black and understandably guarded Ward Eight community how to educate their kids fell on deaf ears. But with honesty and humility, Josh and Lee's credibility gained traction. They attracted eighty students for the school's first semester in the fall of 2001. Josh and Lee, while eager for progress, were also prudent. They understood how their school's long-term success was far from guaranteed. The other education options in Anacostia were not working; still some people weren't holding their breath for change.

"I am confident. I never doubted that I could do this. I never doubted it. But I don't consider myself courageous," replied Josh, when asked about opening the school. "But the truly courageous are the students and teachers. I am a non-conformist, but I am not courageous. I heard it put this way once: 'It is not one thing we do right one hundred percent of the time but the one hundred things we do right one percent of the time.' So I dove in."

Lee worked hard and long hours with Josh during the school's formation. He then moved on to lead programs at Teach for America, an organization also dedicated to educating America's youth. Josh stayed and continued to work at growing the enrollment of the student body and finding enthusiastic and dynamic teachers. He also moved the school to the building on the corner opposite the metro station.

Josh Kern's laugh is loud and contagious. His office is a mess of paper stacks, ranging from international educational studies to last week's grocery shopping list. Streams of calls and visitors distract Josh minute by minute. His single item focus can be short as he addresses thousands of needs and issues a day. There is no steady pace in his gait or prolonged focus on others. He will give you time and full attention if you are quick and make it count.

Bored and unfulfilled as a legal consultant in a staid and detached law firm, Josh realized there was more he could do to help the world. In part, the drudgery of his life as a corporate attorney clarified the passion of his teenage years. He wanted to give in order to live. As Mark Warren relates in *Fire in the Heart*, a book he wrote about racial injustice, Josh said:

Those high school years were years that I really felt myself develop and become my own person. It took me ten years to get that back. This time in my life and that time in my life were the only two times I felt alive, good about what I was doing, connected in a way that I felt like a whole person. I take it for granted that this is what I do. I made the commitment a long time ago. I find it very fulfilling, very meaningful. It gives my life purpose and it's something that I've come to feel very passionate about as I have gotten immersed into it. I actually think this work has been incredibly beneficial for me because it feeds me in some way. I am trying to articulate why I do it. It is not easy to say [why], but I do know this. I wake up every morning and am excited about the day's work.

"There's a lot of ways you can send a message to kids that 'we don't value you,'" Josh explained. "How you run a school sends a message. We believe in an environment that provides care, concern, and discipline in order for achievement to be realized. We know this works." Every single student of every single graduating class in Thurgood Marshall Academy's history has gone on to college.

The freshman science classroom at Thurgood Marshall is filled with thirteen and fourteen-year-olds stretched out on lab tables and the floor. Working in pairs, they label a life-size paper cutout of the human body—one part heart, one part brains, and one part guts. The students joke and laugh about the task at hand while making sure parts are labeled correctly.

The teacher, a thirty-something woman with pulled back hair and a gleam in her eyes strolls from station to station, encouraging her students to stay on task and ask questions freely. For almost the entire period, these boys and girls keep working, joking with other groups spread around the room, comparing their exhibit to the anatomy textbook, and stepping back to admire their work.

During class time in the halls of this three-story building the floors shine and squeak as you stroll them. The wall art and announcements display awards and events of the school. The corridors quietly echo dreams coming true. After each class period, the halls enliven with young men and women walking from math to debate, English to Spanish, and the past to the future.

There are eight simple rules posted throughout the school known as the "No Brainers". They instruct kindness, respect, honor, discipline, and dedication. The rules are rarely broken in here, a world away from the disregard for order immediately outside this space. The kids who follow these guidelines understand their purpose.

Darrion Willis lived with his working mother in the Ward Eight neighborhood of Washington Highlands. With nine thousand residents, it is the largest neighborhood in the poorest section of Washington D.C. Most of the residents live in public housing projects. It is one of the most violent neighborhoods in the District of Columbia. In 2007, 34 percent of Washington D.C.'s murders were committed in Washington Highlands even as it contained only 1.5 percent of the city's population. Here Darrion and his mother bore constant witness to shootings, beatings, drug use, and abject poverty.

Two miles of gang territory created a daily gauntlet from home to Thurgood Marshall, where Darrion found a place to rest his frightened heart. "Thurgood Marshall Academy feels safe," explained Darrion. "No one is threatened. I joined all kinds of clubs at school so that I stayed late, until after the gangs in front of the metro would be gone. My mom made me be home every night before the streetlights came on, but staying late helped me get from school more easily."

The school sowed seeds of change for Darrion. "One day Supreme Court Justice Steven Breyer came to school and talked with students at an assembly. It was overwhelming and intriguing. I asked him lots of questions and wanted to keep talking with him. He was such an inspiration. I knew then that I wanted to change, no, *enhance* my neighborhood through law and politics."

Thurgood Marshall staff also encouraged students to seek knowledge and understanding outside the school, and sometimes Darrion's fears of the city serendipitously arranged that. "Just by random, one day I went to the Smithsonian Museum to get away from the gangs," said Darrion. "Bullies don't go into the Smithsonian because it is not cool. Here I felt most at peace, internalized my emotions, and built on the idea that I wanted to be a lawyer and government official to help enhance my neighborhood."

James Watkins, now a senior at Bates College in Maine and the valedictorian of Thurgood Marshall class of 2008 knew those same fears.

"Statistically, I should be dead or in jail. That is what my neighborhood is like. People there sell drugs but don't do it because it is fun or cool. It is the easiest way to immediately provide for themselves," shared James. "Getting an education or working nine to five does not pay the overdue power bill that means no heat in two days if you can't get money quickly. So, they do what they have to do in order to survive."

Breaking out of the old and creating a new cycle is challenging. There is generally a trigger, something or someone that inspires the individual to reach for more than survival. For James, it was his mother. "The initial step is the hardest step. Then, you have to get accustomed to the pain of moving toward success," explained James. "This helps you prepare for adversity. I did not want to come to Thurgood Marshall. I did not know anyone there."

"It would have been easier for me to just stay at my local high school, but taking the first step allows you to realize one success on which subsequent successes are built," James continued. "At some point you reach a fulcrum where what lies ahead is easier to accomplish than anything you faced in your past. Realizing the benefits of discipline and a caring educational environment, and then passing all of my classes was that fulcrum for me. I was able to move on in life to a place that is very different from Anacostia. With anything I now face, I believe I can achieve."

Given the real and perceived peril associated with Anacostia and Ward Eight, it is even more remarkable how teachers opt to immerse themselves in Thurgood Marshall. Why do so many talented instructors, young and old, rookies and veterans, create opportunities for kids here instead of in D.C.'s affluent suburbs? What sets these teachers apart?

"They put their hearts out there. They care," explained James. "Every day they come to Ward Eight knowing of its dangers but give everything they have to help us succeed. They do not get paid well and could work in a much more comfortable environment."

"My teachers pushed me. My English teacher, Mrs. Lyons, held me to a high standard," continued James. "She saw leadership qualities in me and did not let me be irresponsible. A certain look or single word from her was all I needed to be reminded of my capabilities and responsibilities."

James and his counselors did not agree about what life should look like after Thurgood Marshall. "My college counselor, Mrs. Mitchell, did not let me take the easy road. I did not want to be the token black guy at a prestigious white college. Five years ago there were very, very few people of color at Bates. Today, there are thirty in my graduating class. This is the best place I could be, and Mrs. Mitchell ended up being right about it."

Long after graduation, Thurgood Marshall students and faculty remain family. Alumni newsletters, trips back home, and the emergency fund Thurgood Marshall has for young college students in need of food or textbooks, aids students. "My academic dean, Mrs. Bobo, and the guidance counselor, Ms. Levine, drove up to Bates, a fourteen-hour drive, to see how I was doing," explained James. "The fact they made that effort is unbelievable. I can't take credit for being where I am today. My teachers and counselors are the ones who helped me get here."

Marielys Garcia is a teacher at Thurgood Marshall Academy. She has taught Spanish for six years and is the Foreign Language Department Chair at only twenty eight years old. Marielys is the daughter of immigrant parents who came to this country to make a better life for their family. She understands the challenges facing her students but cannot fully relate, because she was raised in New York City and attended good public schools there.

"Fully relating to my student's experiences outside of school is not critical," said Marielys. "More importantly, I cannot doubt that these students will succeed just because they come from a bad neighborhood. That would be an injustice to them. We truly do understand that the conditions around Thurgood Marshall are severe. But, these students have dreams and we have dreams for them. We tap into that and set expectations for them to realize these dreams."

"Thurgood Marshall succeeds in large part because our own staff expectations are high and that sentiment impacts and improves the school," Marielys stated. "If you don't work hard you will not get asked back to teach. The lack of tenure protection creates some anxiety but it also levels the playing field and keeps you on your toes."

The teacher staff lounge at Thurgood Marshall is an oxymoron. Teachers gather here every day to discuss best practices, address weakness of programs and themselves, ask for advice, and share worries about students who are struggling. Here, colleagues debate school performance based on test results and classroom vibe rather than critique last night's reality TV show winner.

It takes courage from the administration and the teachers to operate in a self-managed environment *that demands the care of students* above all else. Marielys explained, "We are given the leverage to govern ourselves in an environment that allows you to freely communicate with colleagues and administrators. We are allowed space to present and embrace new ideas. Change and improvements inspire teachers. As a team we push each other forward. And, the ship is being steered with student achievement as the goal."

The structure of Thurgood Marshall radically differs from most public schools where layers of regulations, the sheer size of the institution, and maze-like bureaucracy water down the true face of the goal: students succeeding in class and in life. (See article page 99.) "The Thurgood Marshall foundation is simple: Being successful matters," shared Marielys. "Every day we try to get students to realize their potential and dreams. Every day! They are always well aware of our expectations and realize that we are not going to limit them, and that maybe they themselves are their only limitation. As they get this they become very engaged and energized. They realize their own potential."

Each year in June, as the regular school season winds down, students are asked to prepare a portfolio of their individual activities. "The portfolio is a summary of all that the students have learned through the academic year," Josh explained. "Students say that this requirement is the one that best prepares them for college."

Students are required to pick favorite or meaningful lessons from each of their classes and present these choices to a review board made up of instructors and outside evaluators including retired Washington D.C. lawyers. The review board grades each student on presentation quality, poise, and the meaning of the portfolio to that student. For each child, the intrinsic values of the portfolio process are manifold: developing pride in accomplishment, learning to accept compliments, gaining comfort in public speaking, and organizing a presentation for maximum effect.

In the early summer of 2011, tenth grade student Danica Johnson [name changed] presented her portfolio. Danica spoke of what she learned from English, history, law, math, and other classes. She talked about knowing how the people of Cambodia suffered at the hands of the Khmer Rouge, realizing that life was horrifying because the Khmer Rouge "didn't like people who weren't like them."

She described the challenges of kids growing up in the Middle East based on cultural limitations she learned of while reading *The Kite Runner*. She systematically explained why a circle is not a polygon, given that a pure circle when drawn freehand is not composed of several smaller segments. She expressed concerns about people with borderline personality disorder and realized that the same issues "face people today as they did hundreds of years ago," a position she adopted after reading *Hamlet*.

While she may not have realized she was doing it, fifteen-year-old Danica described how she is becoming one of the next generation's leaders. While discussing the circle versus polygon issue, she described her fascination with "how people argue about simple things like this." When asked why she chose not to set a higher GPA goal at the outset of the year, she spoke of her need for balance and a desire to experience life outside of textbooks.

My personal favorite was her description of how challenging it was to assist the boys' flag football team: "Patience is what you need to deal with men," she observed. When invited to share what she learned from the one and only disciplinary action she incurred, she spoke of "serving my time and learning my lesson." When you compare Danica's one day in detention with the poor decisions of many in her community who serve hard time, it becomes even more apparent that Thurgood Marshall Academy saves lives.

The same week Danica presented her portfolio, students gathered for an assembly announcement that two of eight city-wide tuition scholarships from D.C.'s George Washington University were awarded to Thurgood Marshall Academy seniors Moo Bae and Markus Batchelor. "The entire lunchroom erupted on this announcement," Marielys recalled.

"At the start of class after the assembly a lot of my kids

came in crying. They were so happy and proud; proud of their school. They realized that they too wanted that kind of success and this kind of impact on their community. They saw their future and were excited about the possibilities. It was a very emotional moment for us all. It was a reminder that at the end of the day students want to succeed, and we need to support them."

Students come to Thurgood Marshall in the ninth grade with the average academic skills of fifth and sixth graders. In very short order things get better. Tenth grade test scores at Thurgood Marshall are three times higher than other schools in Ward Eight. The school has the highest overall assessment scores among tenth graders of all open enrollment schools in Washington D.C. The average daily attendance here is 92 percent, which is 40 percent better than neighboring schools. (See article page 101.)

Thurgood Marshall Academy's mission is "to prepare students to succeed in college and to actively engage in our democratic society." Alongside the academic standards and expectations of students, Thurgood Marshall provides an environment to enjoy and participate in a complete high school experience. "We strive to change the trajectory of each student's education" explained Alexandra Pardo, the present executive director. "This includes academics but also all aspects of high school, including athletics, arts, clubs, and other typical high school activities. Our goal is for students to leave here feeling successful and with the tools to succeed at college."

Named one of "America's Best High Schools" by *U.S. News*

and World Report Magazine, Thurgood Marshall boasts four million dollars in scholarships awarded to its graduates over the past few years. Dignitaries like First Lady Michelle Obama, Supreme Court justices, and U.S. senators visit the school and its graduation ceremonies on a regular basis. While it is arguably the best school in the city—and a public charter school that any high school student in the Washington D.C. boundary can attend—there are no students from outside the Ward Eight neighborhood. There are many "normal" reasons for this: it is in an old building; it is in a poor neighborhood; it is in an unsafe part of town; there are no athletic fields; and only black kids go there.

Perhaps there are more compelling reasons why only kids from Ward Eight go to Thurgood Marshall. Perhaps it is the tipping point for students who need it the most and is reserved for them. Maybe the local students who live in the poverty and danger of Ward Eight know best what is needed to improve it.

Four years ago, D.C. public schools ranked 51st in the nation. "In the past four years almost one thousand five hundred kids just from Thurgood Marshall Academy alone are in or have graduated from college," explained Darrion Willis, now a twenty-three-year-old college senior. "That is a ton of new talent now in our area." He continued with his future vision for the area:

> I want to become an elected official to help my hometown. I want to return to Ward Eight and serve my friends and neighbors. I see myself running for office

and creating programs that enhance Ward Eight. Elected officials need to become involved in this evolution and not just the successful finished product. For example, we need to find ways to help people become better parents. My mom taught me responsibility by illustrating and demanding it and, without a father figure, I turned into an open-minded, sincere, and good person. I want to help others, and I believe the first step in my community is creating opportunities for parents to become better mothers and fathers by offering programs that teach and reward better parenting skills.

As Washington D.C. grows and the suburbs flourish, Ward Eight continues to struggle, although exceptions like Thurgood Marshall Academy gain strength. Economic development sits on the back burner of most people's minds. "People are not inspired by buildings that are vacant and falling down, and an environment that is gross," shared Darrion.

"There is a solution, and it is based on the Thurgood Marshall model. When you are in a particular environment you ride the energy of that environment. Thurgood Marshall has a winning energy. That is what I intend to create for my hometown. I now know how great D.C. is and how great my neighborhood can become. Thurgood Marshall Academy, and going away to college, did this for me and is doing it for hundreds more."

Josh Kern sparked a movement by taking a stand. Brave teachers and students take it from there. The benefits from

Thurgood Marshall are infinitely valuable. "My alma mater is a place of good character and morality," continued Darrion.

When you put people in a good place and show that you always will care for them it means all the difference in the world. When I think about Mr. Kern, I think of a guy who passed out pamphlets to a poor community, to grow his vision; a guy who set up an institution of learning, discipline, and kindness in a very hard location. There is really no way to adequately describe my feelings for him and everyone at Thurgood Marshall Academy. I feel like I always have to say thank you. I don't think they know what they have really, really done.

EXCEPTIONAL SCHOOLS

In the book *The Good School* by Peg Tyre, the author examines different components of a school to determine what makes one school or classroom good and another bad. These different elements include length of school day and year, class size, the curriculum required by the district, standardized versus performance testing, and teacher quality.

By analyzing numerous studies, speaking with parents, and observing firsthand how schools work, Tyre concludes that successful schools begin and end with the teacher in the classroom.

For decades in American schools, teacher evaluations were done in-house by a school administrator with the results then locked away in a file cabinet. Whispers in the hallway between fellow teachers were the only peer reviews. Good teachers lamented the effects of bad teachers on students. There was no formal peer improvement process, no purposeful venue for sharing effective techniques or lessons, no direction from immediate superiors, and no plan for significant corrections in performance, except in the most egregious cases. Contracts between school districts and unions also prevented the dismissal of poor teachers.

Exceptional schools do a lot of things different—setting them apart from those that are not effectively educating children. They replace archaic lesson plans with innovative approaches designed to reach today's children.

They massage school years and daily schedules to match what studies reveal as the most efficient for learning. They create physical environments that maximize students' interest and desire to learn. They also institute review and improvement practices to hold teachers accountable, requiring high performance for the children under their leadership.

A charter school creates a diversity of learning options for students and an improved scholastic environment. One key difference between most charter schools and public schools is the role of the union. Charter schools are generally not required to hire union teachers. Personnel practices are different from typical schools.

Presently, there is no absolute blanket of evidence to suggest charter schools outperform regular public schools. Most studies of student test scores and other factors do not find a significant difference between charter and public schools universally. Yet, there is ample evidence to suggest that with teacher review standards, specific charter schools far outpace regular district schools in student performance. Most unions do not allow teacher review standards or the ability to fire a tenured faculty member.

"We think the main reason we have reached our goals is we are constantly reviewing the job we are doing. Our staff practices honest introspection and makes improvements based upon what they learn and discuss among their peers," explained Josh Kern. "We also have a full-time quality assurance person who collects and analyzes student test scores. This makes the teachers' time much more productive as they have credible data with which to work. It is hard work, requiring long hours and a highly collaborative staff that is honestly reflective about their efforts. This is the cornerstone to our success."

Teacher performance reviews are increasingly demanded by parents and community members who seek top education opportunities for their children. Charter schools and other non-traditional options proliferate, school districts suffer financially, and reputations erode when alternative schools outperform regular public schools.

This shift is a driving force toward instructor evaluation protocol. As Dan Goldhaber, professor and researcher of education stated in a *Seattle Times* newspaper editorial, "If schools and teachers unions do not get out in front of the teacher-accountability curve, they both may get run over."

CULTURES OF EDUCATION

Chinese rice farmers work in their paddies from before dawn until dusk, from March through October. During the darker winter months, the same amount of time is spent tending to equipment, rebuilding dikes, and making bamboo baskets. Altogether, they spend over three thousand hours a year tending to their farms. A Chinese proverb illuminates this work ethic: "No one who can rise before dawn three hundred sixty days a year fails to make his family rich."

The complexities of rice growing and harvesting in China mandate a relatively autonomous relationship between the owner of the rice paddy lands and the individual farmer. For centuries the Chinese landowners charged only a flat fee for the land used for paddies, allowing the farming tenant to grow as wisely and profitably as he could.

By contrast, Northern European countries for generations practiced a very seasonal approach to farming amid a feudal system that did not economically reward productivity. A typical day of an eighteenth century farm worker was from dawn to noon, two hundred days a year.

The climate-driven seasonal approach meant a lot of down time in the spring and summer as crops grew. Feudal economics essentially contributed to societies of agrarian slave labor. Workers were not paid by aristocrats based on how much they harvested, rather for time spent in the fields.

Manifestations of these historic work reward relationships unfold every day in universities across the United States. Asian students are regarded as the most industrious. Their grades are statistically higher on a per capita basis than American or European counterparts.

Malcolm Gladwell, in his book *Outliers*, reveals that Asian students outscore others on standardized math tests simply because they work harder to answer all of the questions. The TIMSS math and science assessment test reveals that the highest scores come not from the brightest test taker but the hardest working test taker. How do we know this?

Before opening the test booklet and answering the questions, students are asked to complete a long survey about their family, background, and perceptions of math. This survey can be up to one hundred twenty questions long and is designed to give test evaluators tools to analyze results demographically and culturally. Perhaps the most telling statistic reveals how students who take time to answer all of these pretest questions do the best on the test itself.

American schools are based on the Northern European economic culture. Chinese schools are not. The evidence above shows how high school attendance and hard work are predictors of success.

According to research by Elaine Allensworth and John Eaton, nearly 90 percent of ninth-graders who miss only four days or fewer per semester will graduate. Of those who are absent 15 – 20 days per semester, only one in six will graduate.

Thurgood Marshall Academy has an average attendance rate of 92 percent. It also has a curriculum and code of ethics requiring students to work hard and be accountable. These standards shine in the midst of a Washington D.C. school system with an average attendance rate of 83 percent. Thurgood Marshall sends 100 percent of its graduating seniors on to college.

Firefighter **Jim Adams** standing with his wife Amy for the first time in weeks after surviving third degree burns on nearly 50 percent of his body.

Almost two months after being trapped in a near deadly inferno, **Jim Adams** and J.D. Clevenger hug as Jim leaves the hospital.

KELLEY KALAFATICH

Kelley Kalafatich, pioneer river guide, stuntwoman, and award-winning film producer rows a cataraft over and down a 14-foot wave on Chile's Futaleufu River.

Kelley Kalafatich, now paralyzed from the waist down, in a standing wheelchair on the banks of a river in Montana.

ii

Josh Kern and **Theodora Walker** celebrate her graduation from Thurgood Marshall Academy, where 100 percent of seniors from this inner-city charter high school graduate and go on to college.

Josh Kern and students on the front steps of Washington D.C.'s Thurgood Marshall Academy.

Martha Ryan laughs with a young mother and beneficiary of Homeless Prenatal Program, an organization helping thousands of pregnant women and homeless families off the streets of San Francisco.

Martha Ryan, founder and director of the Homeless Prenatal Program.

Jeff Leeland, founder of Sparrow Clubs, soon after his recovery from a life-threatening illness.

Dameon Sharkey, a special needs student of Jeff Leeland's and an inspiration for Sparrow Clubs, holds Michael Leeland a few months after Michael's successful bone marrow transplant.

A young **Dennis Guthrie** at training prior to his combat tours as a helicopter medic in the Vietnam War.

Veterans of Foreign Wars Surgeon General **Dennis Guthrie,** with his wife Dianne, honored by Vice President Joe Biden.

Brianna Mercado, five years cancer-free, now volunteers at programs designed to enable and empower very sick children.

Dance troupe leader, college student, and teenage cancer survivor **Brianna Mercado** soars through the Bay Area sky.

On the summit of Mt. Everest, **Eric Plantenberg** celebrates the sunrise during his successful fundraising expedition for Pakistani school children.

Eric Plantenberg leads a Freedom Personal Development seminar, inspiring thousands to live their dreams.

MARTHA RYAN, JUDY CRAWFORD, CARRIE HAMILTON, and the Homeless Prenatal Program

Acceptance

Compassion and connection can only be learned if they are experienced. If we want our children to love and accept who they are, our job is to love and accept who we are.

—BRENÉ BROWN

I used to wonder why I would work all week and then go volunteer at a local clinic on my day off, but I always left the clinic inches off the ground. When people volunteer and give they feel so much better.

—MARTHA RYAN

G ale force winds off the Pacific pushed cold and damp through Judy Crawford as if she had no skin. The hot crack pipe high inhaled hours earlier sent her up and away, but now she spiraled down. With her infant son she took refuge, teeth chattering, muscles shaking, and a cold hell breaking loose in her mind. "I need to get warm," she silently screamed, as a wall of her cardboard home ripped off and blew down the block, away from the Golden Gate. She glanced down at Tantrell, her sleeping three-year-old, paced up and down the block, and waited for dawn.

An early morning sun warmed them a few degrees and shined a bright light on their world. Judy's sister who invited her to San Francisco—with hopes of Judy getting clean and taking care of Tantrell—now saw her only when Judy needed money. She was sickened by Tantrell's condition, as were the hundreds of daily pedestrians who stepped over Judy as she slept off a crack trip on a filthy city street.

Finally, people had seen enough and the authorities were called. They found mother and child on the corner and took a screaming baby boy from the only face he really knew. As he was placed into the State of California Child Protective Services vehicle and driven to a hot meal and warm bed, Judy fell to the street, buckled by reality.

A decade later, down the street Carrie Hamilton parked her minivan for the night, moving it from the previous night's spot to keep from being towed. She had driven around for an hour, sketchy and paranoid in the residue of yesterday's meth high. She laid her daughter down in the back, covered her in a couple of worn blankets, and stepped outside into a dark fog.

After a few minutes looking around for some scraps of food or loose change in the gutter Carrie gave up and crawled back into the van, took a seat on the passenger side, and headed on a mental trip to who knows where. She awoke as the sun burned between San Francisco skyscrapers, three hours after morning traffic woke her daughter, who played in the back by herself. She knew that her mom would not wake up for a while.

After a couple handfuls of shoplifted cereal, they walked up the street and panhandled white-collar professionals who pitied the little girl and disdained her mother. For several hours they milked the corner and came away with enough money for some orange juice, a couple of apples, and a small bag of meth.

What clean adults would consider the priority purchase was irrelevant to Carrie. It had been nearly two days since she embraced the sting of speed burning through her and she was starting to shake. As an officer on foot approached they scurried away and headed to the row house where she could buy her salve. When Carrie desperately pressed ten dollars into a dealer's hand, she was thrown against the wall. A pair of handcuffs from the undercover cop and a reading of Miranda rights landed Carrie in a cell, her daughter ripped away as hope faded into the night.

According to the National Center on Family Homelessness, every year hundreds of thousands of American families become homeless, including more than 1.5 million children. (See article page 119.) In San Francisco, hundreds of homeless people each night find temporary relief in an abandoned vehicle, an overflowing shelter, on a fellow addict's couch, or maybe in the cool hard comfort of jail.

Others spend nights, weeks, or years sleeping in an alley or walking back and forth all night waiting for sunlight and a trickle of heat. Some are drug addicts, others are mentally ill, and more still are simply broke—financially and spiritually. Like Judy and Carrie, increasing numbers of women with children end up in and do not escape the cycle of homelessness.

Families are the fastest growing segment of the homeless population.

Follow a random homeless person on the street and bear witness to tragedy. Strangers step over and around them, not missing a beat or a chance to judge. Many turn away from the ones ranting at the noise in their head. Most feel no sympathy for a mother who is high and doing whatever it takes to get high again. Society's disregard renders a pattern of destitution that is similar from one homeless mother to the next. First you lose your sense of responsibility, then your desire, next your dignity, and ultimately your child.

Twenty years ago Judy Crawford moved to San Francisco. She was hoping for a fresh start from habits acquired through a rough childhood, bad choices, and a string of tough luck. She started using again within days of arriving in the Bay Area. For two years Judy lived strung out on the streets of San Francisco. Time and again she gave away precious things to get high; her pride, womanhood, and finally her son. Rock bottom hit when the State came, took her baby, and sent him three thousand miles away to relatives in Wisconsin.

Carrie Hamilton lived a similar life in San Francisco for years. "My drug of choice was meth. I came from a family with substance abusers and left that life hoping to do better in San Francisco," said Carrie. It did not work. She and her daughter lived in a minivan for years.

"To try to make it seem like an adventure as opposed to being homeless, I told my daughter we were camping. We also ended up sleeping on fellow addicts' couches and floors many, many nights. I ended up in jail several times for drug use and other things. However, it was the last time in that something clicked. I knew I had to change. I had reached bottom."

On the first day they left behind their respective pasts, Judy and Carrie each woke up alone, broken down, and without their children. Both needed help and sought grace to change from a life of sleeping on the street with their babies. Both found salvation in the form of Martha Ryan.

As one of thirteen children raised in an Irish Catholic family, Martha grew up poor in San Mateo, California. Donations from her Catholic school at times fed the family. One Christmas when Martha was a child, two philanthropic strangers knocked on their door and gave the Ryans two bags of toys. This allowed the kids to escape the feeling that Santa might be punishing them for bad behavior.

Even bare necessities were scarce. One cold winter morning, the woman driving the school carpool came to pick up Martha and her brothers and sisters. "My mother told her Tim, my oldest brother, was not going," recalled Martha. "When asked if he was sick, my mom replied 'No, he can't find his other shoe.'"

In her early twenties Martha moved to Africa where she worked as a nurse, educating the women of small villages in Somalia about preventive health care. There she developed a true community approach to health care—where all mothers, sisters, and strangers worked together.

In the late 1980s Martha moved back to the U.S. to earn a full nursing degree. While volunteering at a local community health clinic she befriended pregnant homeless women. Martha noticed how priorities quickly shifted among most pregnant women, from a focus on getting high to getting straight. She realized how the power of pregnancy had great potential to transform women from homeless substance abusers or perpetual victims of physical abuse to strong, caring, and successful mothers. She applied for a grant to start a program upon this precept and to her surprise, received it. With expert advice from fellow medical practitioners, social workers, and the sponsor of the grant, she started the Homeless Prenatal Program in 1990.

The Homeless Prenatal Program is located in a typical San Francisco mixed-use commercial neighborhood, with rundown buildings, barred windows, and people standing on corners waiting for a bus or light or something to change. Inside the center, things are different. It is bright and alive and change is taking place.

I first met Martha Ryan in the summer of 2011 in her office at the Homeless Prenatal building on the second floor mezzanine, which overlooks the open first floor. The center is decorated with orange, yellow, and bright blue walls and display boards with photos of smiling children and happy mothers. Offices with open doors provide counseling, cooking classes, job skills, and prenatal care. Martha greeted me with a warm smile, a soft twinkle in her eye, and a firm handshake.

Martha upholds the hope of many women with no other place to go. "I realized the state of pregnancy was a wonderful window of opportunity for a woman to turn her life around," explained Martha. "They needed more than just prenatal care. They needed housing. They needed help with addiction. Some needed to get away from a batterer. They had lived their lives in poverty and they needed help to overcome these barriers."

While Martha recognizes the random and unpredictable causes of homelessness, she also understands its recurring patterns from one generation to the next. "Poverty is an accident at birth; children don't get to choose which families they are born into," shared Martha. "But regardless of how it happens, people who are born into poverty or raised in poverty have fewer opportunities than those that are born into a family of means."

"In 1989 I was a volunteer nurse working at a homeless shelter," recalled Martha. "I went out one evening onto the streets and there were three women at different stages of pregnancy and not one was getting prenatal care." Martha drew on her experience in remote third world countries and compared it to the streets of San Francisco.

"I had planned to return to Africa to set up maternal child health programs in the developing world, and little did I know that there was a developing world right here in San Francisco." She took her Africa experience one step further. "The Homeless Prenatal Program is modeled after work I did in refugee camps in Africa. In the camps we trained women to be health care providers. At Homeless Prenatal we train former homeless mothers as community health workers."

"I used to wonder why I would work all week and then go volunteer at a local clinic on my day off, but I always left the clinic inches off the ground," shared Martha. "When people volunteer and give they feel so much better. It is so easy to cast judgment on someone that you don't know. And if we could just not do that and accept people for who they are and be nice and kind and give a helping hand, we'd feel better about life and so would everybody else."

The Homeless Prenatal building is staffed with individuals who don't let their head hit the pillow at night without making a difference. "When I got out of jail for the last time, it was Homeless Prenatal that gave me the opportunities to help myself," shared Carrie. "More than anything, I did not feel judged here and got the support—emotional, physical, and financial—that no one else had given me. They helped me realize that I was worth something and helped me know that I could make a much better life for my daughter."

Over half of the people working at Homeless Prenatal have overcome lives of drug addiction, abuse, or homelessness and now counsel and help others as they were helped. Judy's first legitimate steps to recovery and providing a better life for her son started with Homeless Prenatal.

"I was an addict for years, and could not escape that cycle," explained Judy. "My son was taken from me by the State and placed with relatives. I got arrested. I spent a lot of nights out in the cold. I remember many, many times just walking back and forth, all night, waiting for the sun and for it to warm up." After hitting bottom Judy sought redemption. "I am not proud of that time but I came through it. I found this place [Homeless Prenatal] and got turned around."

Judy and Carrie are now full-time counselors at Homeless Prenatal. Their empathy and understanding was born on the experience side of the fence. "What made the difference for me, and what I do now, is not judging people when they walk through the door. They listened and now I listen," explained

Judy. "They didn't preach to me and tell me what to do. They cared, and they gave me hope and ideas. That is what I do now, being on this end of things and knowing what it is like without someone who accepts you and really tries to help."

When the Homeless Prenatal Program front door swings open, the cold coastal air brings an unsteady family with it. A ragged man, shell-shocked woman and two wary children meekly approach the front counter. The attendant smiles gently and says hello in front of a big colorful backdrop separating the lobby from the inner workings of this sanctuary. With head bowed, the man quietly explains how their car with all their belongings was towed away.

He asks for overnight housing for his wife and kids. The staffer explains that there is no housing at this location, but she is confident they will be able to help. As she passes the father a short form to complete, the mom and kids listen to soft sounds of hope coming from the other side of the wall. After just a few minutes, the family is ushered through the doors and into the heart of the place where those sounds are no longer muffled.

There is only one front door here. It is safer for women seeking shelter from abusive men, and for families to rest in complete security and recover from the perils of the street. Those who come through the door are frail-bodied, trampled souls. For many, this is their final opportunity to get help and get right, whether led by the hand of God or by the long arm of the law.

The family sits down in an office with bright walls and announcements tacked up on bulletin boards. Notebooks line one wall and a desk with a computer takes up space. Physical luxuries like big, convenient rooms are not available here, but spiritual rewards abound. Alongside the core office spaces, larger rooms house a child's playroom, sewing class, birth training space, and a computer lab.

Judy Crawford walks in and introduces herself, extending a welcoming hand to the family. After listening for fifteen minutes, Judy suggests the kids head down the hall to the playroom. They step in to meet another counselor who walks them over to a table of blocks. The five and seven-year-old pick up the colorful squares and start to build a house.

Judy arranges temporary housing for the family's next few nights and gives them a time to return the next day for food and community. The steps beyond this are not solidly outlined but Judy encourages the man and woman to accept that someone cares, a way out is possible, and help is here. A journey of new beginnings always starts with one step.

Over the next few weeks the husband is equipped with work options, the mother is provided with longer-term housing opportunities to consider for the family, and the kids laugh and play. "The first step is to let people know that they are in a place where they can feel trust no matter where they came from. People like me on the streets are always judged poorly," said Judy. "This place just doesn't do that. That is why it works. From there we help take care of other basic needs in order for survival to be less of a concern and getting better to become a priority."

Physical and emotional needs are tended to. "My counselor at Homeless Prenatal helped me find housing and inspired me to apply for job training that led to a position doing community outreach," recalled Carrie. "More than programs and jobs though, she gave me resolve and strength to stay in recovery and find purpose for myself and my family. Today, I try to do the same for those that walk through our door."

Two thousand San Francisco families found permanent housing in the past five years, thanks to Homeless Prenatal. This means that more than a family a day came off the streets and into a home, at a time when government-run programs were being slashed. Carrie explained why it is crucial for Programs like Homeless Prenatal to stick around:

> Social services are first on the budget chopping block. It may just be a line on a list for policymakers and voters, but for a homeless mom, it's a bed for her family or the help she needs. For a newborn baby, it's the way out of the cycle of homelessness and addiction. Behind the balance sheets and politics of government spending are the lives of real people—people who need help to be independent and live constructive lives of purpose and meaning… No matter how bad it is we help people find reasons to believe in living and succeeding. We help them understand this—their children deserve to be healthy and to know they are as beautiful as any other is.

Homeless Prenatal successfully helps homeless families transition from destitution to promise by arranging for and providing housing. They give pregnant women a safe haven to come off drugs and the streets through peer counseling and mentor education. They also offer job training and place-ment services to help build lives of purpose and self-reliance. Homeless Prenatal Program's mission statement and organi-zational values underscore why this program is working:

> In partnership with our families, we break the cycle of childhood poverty. By seizing the motivational oppor-tunity created by pregnancy and parenthood, HPP joins with families to help them recognize their strengths and trust in their capacity to transform their lives.

> We believe that people can change and they want a better life for themselves and their children.

> Every mother wants to deliver a healthy baby and become a good parent.

> We are committed to providing a non-judgmental, motivating and empowering environment that builds trust and strengthens the family.

> We show respect to every client and treat them with empathy and compassion.

> We are committed to providing a culturally sensitive environment and services to all families.

> We recognize that people have strengths and do not need to depend on us or any other agency or system.

We never give up on anyone; they are always welcome to come back.

We believe in the importance of building a sense of community among families who have no other source of support.

HPP honors diversity and respects the culture and dignity of each family.

In San Francisco today, government-run social programs cost the city approximately sixty thousand dollars per homeless person a year. The Homeless Prenatal Program, with an annual budget of approximately six million dollars, helps break the cycle of poverty and homelessness for less than five thousand dollars per person, with over two thousand four hundred families served each year.

The program is funded through a mix of grants, donations, and government funds. It saves money for our local, state, and national government while adding healthy and productive families to society. Over half of its sixty employees were former clients and homeless individuals, or substance abusers. What Martha Ryan created transforms the individual from within.

Since its inception, the Homeless Prenatal Program has placed over three thousand six hundred families in permanent housing, meaning over ten thousand kids and parents no longer endure the despair of homelessness. Nearly two hundred new families seek help from Homeless Prenatal for the first time each month. Homeless Prenatal counsels thousands of mothers and fathers out of the world of drugs and into work. They provide countless children a healthy environment to grow and develop in.

Much of the Homeless Prenatal Program's success is due to cash and in-kind donations from companies and individuals. (See article page 121.) Businesses like Wells Fargo, Chevron, Gap, Levi Strauss, and other large corporations see the philanthropic and economic benefits that Homeless Prenatal provides to communities. When parents become productive members of society rather than users of government assistance, politicians and government officials recognize the fiscal and societal improvements.

Individuals, businesses, and governments give as a two-way street. Homeless Prenatal improves lives and communities. When more people contribute to the economic cycle instead of taking from it, the whole world is lifted. Micro and macroeconomies flourish from producing members of society via their purchasing and taxpaying power. Fewer people are dependent on government handouts or others to keep them fed and in homes. The cycle of poverty on an individual, family, and community level, meets a benevolent roadblock at Homeless Prenatal.

"We do this because if the family stays on the street, if the parents remain addicted, if the parents continue to abuse the children, if the parents continue to neglect their children, then the child does not stand a chance," said Martha. "The child will become like the parents because that is all the child knows."

"All I knew about raising kids was the way that I was raised," expressed client Venetta Coffman. "Coming up through the

Homeless Prenatal Program, after a while you see that your parents yelling at you all the time and hitting you all the time just wasn't the way. That's the way they were raised. Well, I am getting different things and hopefully my kids will get even more than that. Hopefully, the buck stops here."

"The staff here make me feel like part of a family," shared client Beth Peterson who was homeless with two children. "They make you feel safe again."

"This place saved me and helped me get back my son. I have a good job and my own home, which is a long way from where I was," said Judy. "I was given love and a chance at the Homeless Prenatal Program, and made to feel worthwhile. Now I am stronger, help other people that were in the same situation as me, and teach my son how to succeed. I do it all one day at a time."

Judy and Carrie made an end a beginning. The Homeless Prenatal Program's heart of acceptance helped them take the first steps up. The warmth of support and rebuilt self-esteem enabled their growth. With their kids, they now start their days desiring to make a positive difference. Dozens like Judy and Carrie at Homeless Prenatal spread rays of kindness and give life back to the despaired. And all it took was Martha Ryan—one single caring and courageous person—to change the world.

FAMILY HOMELESSNESS

Family homelessness in America is an often-ignored epidemic. As detailed by the National Center on Family Homelessness:

Every year, hundreds of thousands of American families become homeless, including more than 1.5 million children. These children are hidden from our view, but they are living in shelters, cars, and campgrounds. They are young and scared, and their parents and families are frustrated and desperate.

The fastest growing segment of the homeless population is families. The effects of family homelessness on children are statistically and emotionally staggering. Again, according to the National Center on Family Homelessness, homeless children are twice as likely to be expelled or drop out of high school.

Homeless children are four times more likely to have developmental challenges. Reading and math skill scores are 16 percent lower among homeless children than their counterparts with homes. They have twice the amount of moderate to serious health issues as other children. Children without a home also worry much more than other kids that something bad will happen to their family.

From 2007 to 2009 homelessness climbed at an astronomical rate. High unemployment, significant underemployment, and the reduction in municipal and state funds for homeless programs led to a 10 to 60 percent jump in homelessness, depending on location.

While there are federal programs designed to improve employment opportunities, in modern history only one piece of legislation specifically geared toward homelessness was approved.

The McKinney-Vento Homeless Assistance Act of 1987 helped provide funds for shelters, job training, health care and other services for the homeless. Even with the significant increases in homelessness over the past few years, no homeless-specific federal assistance was voted in. The problem is growing and public funds are shrinking.

An outcome of this epidemic is an increase in programs and homeless shelters privately funded through charities, churches, and individual and institutional donations. Many centers have opened in recent years to help with the immediate need. Others like Martha Ryan's have long existed, knowing that the problem will continue as long as inequities, mental illness, and substance abuse remain.

While many programs effectively deal with the symptoms by providing shelter and food, the staff and volunteers at the Homeless Prenatal Program strike at the root causes of family homelessness and work tirelessly to address and remedy those issues.

AMERICA GIVING

Organizations like the Homeless Prenatal Program are dependent on donations for survival. Half of their annual six-million-dollar budget comes from cash and in-kind donations.

On a national level, in 2010, approximately three hundred billion dollars were donated to nonprofits in the form of cash and in-kind gifts. This represents an increase since 2008 and 2009 when charitable contributions took a huge hit from national economic challenges.

Approximately 35 percent of all charitable contributions go to churches and other religious organizations. Education services receive 14 percent and human services, 9 percent. The least funded categories include environmental and animal rights organizations. Homeless Prenatal Program is considered a human services nonprofit organization.

The demographics of the donors are most striking. Ninety-five percent of all charitable contributions come from individuals, bequests, and private foundations. Only 5 percent of all donations to nonprofits come from corporations. Furthermore, the top giving corporations in the U.S. contribute approximately 1 percent of their gross income to nonprofit causes.

In 2009, Wal-Mart—the top U.S. corporation in gross sales and total dollars donated—had net sales of $401 billion and an operating income of $22.8 billion. Yet it donated less than $288 million as a company. Wal-mart's net sales increased 7.2 percent, while its charitable contributions *decreased* 10 percent.

In recent history, the top corporate giver as a ratio of income is Target Corporation. Target donates approximately 2 percent of its gross income to nonprofits, focusing largely on educational entities. This ratio is far more in keeping with what individual Americans give.

While corporate donations are significant in terms of gross dollar amounts, the ratio of giving is half of what American individuals contribute. According to the IRS and various studies, charitable contributions from individuals in the past twenty years range from 1.5 to 2.2 percent of their income.

Americans give nearly twice as much as the second most philanthropic country, Britain, and seven times more than the French. By class, Americans give disproportionately to charities. Low-income families donate approximately 4.5 percent of their income compared to 3 percent among high-income families.

If corporations matched the ratio of individual giving (rounded to 2 percent of income) the total annual increase in contributions to nonprofits would be approximately fifteen billion dollars.

This would fund two thousand five hundred more organizations like the Homeless Prenatal Program and help hundreds of thousands of homeless families across the country. The sustainability of corporations relies on a healthy and productive society. When corporations give back to individuals, hope is secured in the economy of the future.

JEFF LEELAND and SPARROW CLUBS

Compassion

———— ∞ ————

The heart of the giver makes the gift dear and precious.
— MARTIN LUTHER KING, JR.

Compassion is always there, to be given and to receive.
It is the hand, heart, and hope of God.
—JEFF LEELAND

This drive to the hospital seemed much longer than the trip just two weeks earlier. The coughing was more ragged, the fever was higher, breaths were very shallow, and the sobbing too painful. Michael Leeland was in pain and too young to describe what he felt, but his parents Jeff and Kristi knew this spell was more severe. Their five-month-old was not getting rid of what made him seem a little sick a few weeks earlier and landed him at the emergency room fourteen days ago. Now he was even more feverish and could not catch his breath. Michael was getting worse.

They sat for just a few minutes in the waiting room. Crying babies tug at the heart strings of even the most hardened hospital admission clerks. They moved to an inner room, sat behind the curtain, and watched nurses check Michael's temperature and heart-rate that was racing to pump freshly oxygenated blood through his sick fifteen-pound body. Antibiotics were ordered again on this visit, despite their temporary effect last time. This time a blood test was ordered too.

Jeff held his trembling son close even though his own body heat made cooling Michael's temperature more difficult. The first needle poke shot Michael's screams through Jeff and Kristi's hearts as the antibiotic coursed its way in. The next, targeted for a vein, missed its mark. The blood sample did not draw. Another stab missed again. Michael wailed louder.

Jeff hugged him tighter as Kristi held her face in her hands, until finally needle found vein and blood filled the syringe. After weeks of doctor and hospital visits without an effective diagnosis, the Leelands hoped that the test would provide something tangible to fix. As midnight crept in the Leelands headed home and Michael fell asleep as the ibuprofen cooled him and fatigue won over.

A few days later Jeff and Kristi were asked to come to the doctor's office as soon as possible. The diagnosis was a gut punch: leukemia. White blood cells were being destroyed, leaving Michael vulnerable to illness and unable to fight infection. The Leelands slumped and prayed for help from God, wondering why and waiting for the oncologist to explain the next steps.

Treating infant leukemia is a very long process with no guarantee of survival, especially with Michael's more deadly variety of the disease. A bone marrow transplant was imperative to give him any chance. Michael needed to undergo days of body core-stripping radiation to eradicate all of the blood cells in his body—the few remaining good along with the bad. More chemotherapy would attack any vestige of illness that might survive the radiation. Then the tedious marrow transplant process could begin. But first Michael needed an exact marrow donor match. The Leelands left the office in silence, save for the sound of their tears.

The complex marrow compatibility matrix typically requires an exhaustive search of family, relatives, and strangers for a match. Jeff and Kristi were tested but not compatible. Michael's three older siblings—Jaclyn, Amy, and Kevin—were tested next. As Michael battled time and continued to suffer from respiratory infections and high temperatures, amazingly a match was found: Amy. The smallest of imaginable donors had the marrow that Michael needed. A miracle took the form of a six-year-old who would suffer to save her brother.

The Leelands had just moved to Seattle. Jeff was hired as a junior high school athletic director and teacher. He previously worked in a small Eastern Washington town and struggled with the decision to move to a bigger city, but he and Kristi knew the move would benefit their family. Jeff's pay was higher, the insurance plan more comprehensive, and professional growth opportunities were available.

Jeff's position as a school teacher afforded options and benefits that many do not have. His job was secure. He had the administration's blessing to take time off to be a father to his very sick child. Also, Jeff's new group insurance policy provided ample coverage for Michael's transplant, preventing financial disaster and granting the life-saving treatment Michael needed. Or so he thought.

Michael's condition deteriorated as cancer weakened his ability to fight infection. The hospital assisted Jeff to prepare the necessary documents for insurance coverage of the procedures, which would cost over two hundred thousand dollars. Jeff contacted the insurance company for approval.

Jeff was employed in the new school district for only six months when he made the insurance request. Twelve months of employment was required to satisfy the "transplant waiting period clause." The Leelands were denied coverage. Jeff and Kristi pleaded, then boiled over. Michael did not have time to wait, and they had no money to pay for the life-saving procedure. They asked themselves how this could happen. How could an insurance company deny coverage for a treatment to save Michael's life?

"Our initial hope was that the cancer would not progress too rapidly, as we knew the insurance would cover the transplant and other costs if we could do it in October, when the one-year waiting period expired," explained Jeff. "But the disease progressed and we knew Michael would not make it." Michael was a five-month-old victim of a system that tried to place a monetary value on saving his life.

Because the Leelands were not citizens of a country with comprehensive health care protections, and as insurance companies still recovered from massive investment losses in the 1980s recession, the insurance company refused to pay for Michael's procedure. (See article page 141.)

The clinical impact of this policy was obvious. Michael

and others like him would die in the name of a balance sheet. The emotional impact goes without saying. Jeff believed he had failed his most important job—to let no harm come to his children. "It was very tough during this time of our lives," explained Jeff. "I was mad, distraught and had moments of self-pity."

Michael was admitted again as his condition worsened. Jeff spent nights at the hospital while Kristi stayed at home with the other children. In the mornings, Jeff went to work and Kristi came to the hospital to be with Michael. Despite sleep deprivation every day, Jeff summoned strength to teach physical education classes. The roll call of his Adaptive Physical Education class included one child bound to a wheelchair by a neurological disorder, another unable to speak from a severe learning disorder, and more still with serious physical and developmental constraints.

"There were so many kids who just wanted to be normal and accepted. One boy, Danny, was a sports fanatic but confined to a wheelchair," remembered Jeff. "Another, Dameon, was a really big kid with learning disabilities and some physical limitations due to his size. Dameon had very few friends because of his differences. I made him my assistant because I believed it would give him a purpose and help his pride."

Every day, when the other students ran laps around the basketball court, Dameon proudly pushed Danny around so he could do the laps too. Jeff recalled, "After class one day, Dameon walked up to me and said, 'You know, Mr. Leeland, we have a lot to be thankful for. It could be a lot worse'. I will always remember that day. I still was in the middle of trying to save my son, but Dameon's attitude and comment helped keep things in perspective, and does to this day."

Still, anger welled inside Jeff. "I remember driving to school feeling so hopeless and upset," said Jeff. "There were times I just wanted to chuck my keys on the principal's desk and walk away." Instead, he met with Principal Steve Mezich at Kamiakin Junior High, and let his heart bleed. Steve explained in Jeff's book *One Small Sparrow*:

> On a Wednesday morning Jeff stepped into my office, closed the door, and began to update me on the insurance situation with Michael. Clearly he was drained of all physical and emotional energy. His family was working on its last five hundred dollars, but Jeff was not looking for anything. He just needed someone to listen.
>
> Jeff had to leave school to attend to another matter. That afternoon before I started our regular Wednesday staff meeting, I put off the agenda for a moment to tell the staff about Jeff's situation. I felt compelled that we as colleagues do something immediately to help. That was the most emotional staff meeting I have ever been in.
>
> The staff started talking about what to do and when all the dust settled we had a pretty formal plan. The most heartwarming thing for me was the rallying of Jeff's colleagues. A phenomenal energy poured out of that meeting.

Two days later Jeff sat alone in his office. Dameon and his mother walked in. Dameon stuck out his hand and said,

"Mr. Leeland, you're my partner. And if your little boy's in trouble I'm going to help you out." Then with a proud mom's approval, Dameon handed Jeff 12 five-dollar bills—he'd emptied his entire bank account. As Jeff said, "Sixty dollars you wouldn't change for a million." Dameon shared this gift in his own words, also in *One Small Sparrow*:

I still remember meeting Mr. Leeland. I was your young, lovable kid. I was standing in the background, watching the kids play sports, when this young guy comes over and says "You're Dameon Sharkey?" "Well, yeah," I say. "Why do you ask?" "I'm your teacher," he says. He makes me get up, and then he says "Dameon, I'm gonna get you in shape even if it kills you."

When you see one P.E. teacher, you've seen them all. But this guy put the hook in me. I still hold him in the highest regard. Mr. Leeland helped me a lot. Basically, he is my mentor. If it wasn't for him, well…if I ever get married, I'll ask Mr. Leeland to be my best man.

Anyway, one Friday they were passing out flyers about Michael and I'm reading this and thinking "All right, this guy has helped me through a lot. He pulled me though a lot of rough stuff." So I sort of ran out to the car and said "Mom, I've gotta go to the bank. I've gotta wipe out my entire savings account. I've gotta give this to Mr. Leeland."

"Now wait a minute, wait a minute, slow down," she said. "Just hold it. Why?" "You know Mr. Leeland?" I asked her. "Yeah, you told me about him," she said. "Well, I want to give him my sixty dollars for his little boy because he needs a bone marrow transplant."

To make a long story short, we go up to his office fifteen minutes later, I hand him sixty dollars, and I say to him, "The only thing I want from you is a thank you and a smile." Basically, that's what happened. It was the greatest thing I ever did.

The students of Kamiakin Junior High created fundraising movements at school. Teachers gave money to the Leelands. They shared with their students the grave situation and created curriculum around it. They took a stand and galvanized a community to provide for one of its own. Grace was unbound.

The entire student body rallied for the cause. Optimistic teachers and idealistic students felt injustice had been brought to the Leelands through the insurance company's rejection of the claim for Michael's transplant. A can-do approach replaced bitterness as students created fundraising activities to cover what the insurance company would not. A special bank account was opened for donations.

Students, with teacher's guidance, came up with dozens of plans. Car washes, bake sales, walkathons, and more ideas were met with enthusiastic support throughout the school. Each idea and activity grew wings. A community service program was born and magic was made.

The news media took up the story and aired it around the country. Donations from across the U.S. poured in, catching the Leelands and Kamiakin completely by surprise. Some days literally tens of thousands of dollars arrived by mail at the bank. Students were sent to the branch to help the staff open envelopes and sort the donations. From May 15 to June 12, over $227,000 was raised through student-driven community support efforts.

At the end of each school year Kamiakin Junior High holds an awards assembly. That year, Dameon was called to the floor for a special award. "As Dameon was introduced, he received a standing ovation," Jeff recalled. "The entire auditorium was on their feet cheering. Here was a kid that had few real connections with friends at school, as he was outwardly different. Everyone leaving that gym knew why the 'target' of Kamiakin had become the hero!"

Dameon was saluted as a school leader with the "Character Award" for demonstrating the most concern of all students at Kamiakin. "Dameon later said to me, 'Mr. Leeland, you wouldn't believe how many girls want to talk to me now!'" Jeff shared. "I realized how important his giving and caring was to him and others, and the difference it made in his life."

With the fundraising money Michael's procedures could begin. Killing all of his blood cells meant that good and bad were both destroyed. Very painful sores appeared all over Michael's body. Amy's marrow was extracted and given to Michael by a transfusion. Ongoing blood tests that measure white blood cell counts monitored the success of the transplant. The marrow transplant process required Michael's complete isolation from human touch to prevent infection. Plastic-sheathed walls, sterile face masks, and barrier gloves separated Michael from his parents during his tenth and eleventh months of life.

The critical blood count reports came in, wildly fluctuating at first. Hopes raised and lowered every day. High counts meant the marrow was taking. Low counts indicated problems including possible rejection. Jeff and Kristi lived by the numbers, day after day. Finally, the counts stabilized at a perfectly high number. Michael's new marrow was working well; he was free to leave the isolation room behind the plastic wall. His grandfather described Michael, still less than a year old, "sitting in his mother's lap and touching her face because for so long there had been no contact, no skin on skin. He just couldn't keep his hands off her. He had to touch her."

Today Michael is a thriving twenty-something and the Leelands are forever changed. The courage of the Kamiakin community created an energy that lives on. Jeff marveled at the movement and founded a program modeled on his school's benevolence—the Sparrow Clubs. After a few more years of teaching and building the program, in 1996 Jeff resigned from teaching and dedicated his life to Sparrow Clubs.

Sparrow Clubs honor countless other children who need help with a simple formula based on the response to Michael's crisis. It is simply *kids helping kids.* Sparrow Clubs inspired by Dameon's compassion and single act of kindness. "He once remarked to me that he understood why Columbine happened," Jeff explained. "He knew the pain of isolation and disregard that those students had felt. He also knew that kids generally go one of two ways in a school environment."

Sparrow Clubs believe that kids in school both need support and need to support others. "I witnessed the problems that Dameon had and then recognized the benefits Dameon received. As an isolated kid with physical and emotional issues of his own, he found something to live for, something to give," said Jeff. "And so I just built on that."

Some kids hurt more than others as they navigate the maze of adolescence, but all have significant needs as they cross from childhood to adulthood. Providing teenagers something to believe in and work toward teaches them the valuable lesson of giving to a cause greater than themselves. This in turn buoys their confidence and sense of worth. "This process builds sanctuaries where kids can feel good about themselves, offsetting many of the negatives that they face every day," said Jeff.

Sadly, Dameon passed away in 2000 from a staph infection that overwhelmed his body and attacked his organs. His legacy lives on in the form of the Sparrow Clubs, the growth and impact of which he witnessed in his final years. It was Dameon who suggested the idea that Sparrow Clubs provide a sanctuary to kids. The Sparrow Clubs' mission statement and charter says best how everyone in a school benefits from the organization:

Sick kids get help. Healthy kids become heroes. Schools become sanctuaries.

Sparrow Clubs USA is a national nonprofit organization of school-based clubs that assist children in medical crisis. Through community service and fundraising projects, Sparrow Clubs support children who have either life-threatening illnesses or chronic disabilities and whose families face financial hardship because of it.

Individual schools and youth groups are paired

with a qualified local child, often a classmate, who is facing a medical crisis. Sparrow Clubs offer young people a way to aid one another. Along with the day-to-day agenda of academics, when a whole school rallies to help one particular child in crisis, the students learn as much from this "hidden curriculum of caring as an institutional pattern and practice, as they do from the formal curriculum of concepts and facts" [Parker Palmer]. The adoption of a Sparrow sets the stage for caring, empathy and simple yet heroic acts of kindness to be played out in ways that positively change an entire school community.

Sparrow Clubs facilitate this by matching local children in medical need/crisis with neighborhood schools and young people who "adopt" the child and family. Local businesses and corporations support both the child and the school by pledging seed money to sponsor Sparrow Club projects. Ultimately, Sparrow Clubs do much more than simply provide financial and emotional support for critically ill children and their families.

By allowing youth who are personally hurting to help medically needy kids, Sparrow Clubs' unique service learning model empowers youth to transform feelings of purposeless, detachment and anger, into confidence, solidarity and compassion.

As they state, Sparrow Clubs help kids "find their wings" and rise above their own difficulties by helping others.

Every child has a gift. Sparrow Clubs help each one find it. We believe that kids can do heroic things...but they need heroic things to do. With rising violence, drug abuse, teenage pregnancy and despair among our nation's youth, it is critically important that we provide them with meaningful experiences that give purpose, teach compassion, and instill character, dignity and a sense of community. Sparrow Clubs accomplish this through service learning opportunities that let kids discover the hero and gifts that are within themselves, by helping local children in medical need.

From 2001 to 2010, hundreds of families and their Sparrows received millions of dollars in financial assistance. Tens of thousands of collective kid hours of community service were performed to earn cash for and provide help to needy families. Local businesses and individuals throughout the country dig deep each year to donate to the Sparrow Clubs. Every day someone's life is touched through this organization.

Jeff wrote another book—*Disarming the Teenage Heart*—in which he describes the "heroic capacities hidden in the hearts of teens" such as compassion, courage, character, and conscience. He illustrates with Sparrow Clubs how teens equipped with the right tools make right decisions to help others.

I mentioned to a friend of mine who is on the Sparrow Clubs board of directors that I was writing a book and planned to include a chapter on Jeff and Sparrow Clubs. I was hooked as a donor at a Sparrow Club fundraiser a few years earlier, where Jeff spoke of Michael's fight and the evolution of his organization. My friend shared with me that Jeff was struggling. His life had become unbalanced during the preceding two years. Sparrow Clubs was still providing great service but was challenged by far fewer donations because of the economy. Jeff was suffering from depression and illness. He was no longer the executive director of Sparrow Clubs.

Several weeks later, I met with Jeff Leeland in an intensive care unit. My friend thought that my visiting and sharing with Jeff about his story might buoy his spirits. Jeff lay in the hospital bed, feverish, lungs hacking, and struggling to breathe. After trying to speak with him for two minutes, his nurse ushered us out as we watched Jeff's oxygen count plummet. The next day he was airlifted to a larger regional hospital; he could no longer breathe on his own.

During the ensuing days and weeks in intensive care his heart stopped, brain swelled and breathing was performed by a ventilator. He lay in a coma for days, with doctors unable to diagnose his illness. Death hung in the air as lung biopsies revealed an unknown autoimmune disease attacking his body. His doctors could not identify the cause of his life-threatening condition or how to fix it.

The path that led Jeff to this state is a study in compassion gone awry. In the spring of 2009, Sparrow Clubs had fallen on hard times. Disposable income across the country had largely dried up, and donations to nonprofits were drastically reduced. At Sparrow Clubs, staff hours were reduced but positions weren't completely eliminated. Jeff, realizing his salary was a drag on the organization, offered to quit and provide services on a volunteer basis. Even this was not enough. Jeff and Kristi began supporting Sparrow Clubs with their savings.

At the same time, the need of Sparrows grew as more and more parents became unemployed and children got sick. Jeff and Sparrow Clubs continued providing services so that schools could adopt new Sparrows. The financial impact on Jeff and Kristi grew heavier, and their marriage suffered. With no income, Jeff's dreams of the Sparrow Clubs' unlimited availability to those in need were crumbling. As his life unraveled—by his own admission—he turned to alcohol to relieve the pain.

The downward spiral continued when Jeff was arrested for driving under the influence. It grew worse when the Sparrow Clubs' board of directors asked him to step down from his position. Others stepped in to lead the organization that Jeff had lovingly built; Steve Mezich became the executive director.

As Jeff's principal at Kamiakin, Steve had helped grow the program from the start. "Jeff gave everything he had to the Sparrow Clubs. In fact, he gave too much," shared Steve during Jeff's hospitalization. "His desire to keep it running was all-consuming. Sparrow Clubs was built on his vision and desire, and he was unable to watch it struggle. One of his greatest strengths—tireless determination to care for others—blinded him to taking care of himself. We pray for Jeff. The world is a much better place because of him."

Six weeks after witnessing his struggle for breath—nearly a month of which he spent in the intensive care unit—I sat down with Jeff for lunch. He was two weeks removed from the hospital and thirty-some pounds lighter. Though he was never precisely diagnosed and given a specific remedy, Jeff took a drastic detour from death to breathe on his own again. Courtesy of time, good care, and the grace of God, he was healed.

Jeff's hands shook from a strong dose of steroids prescribed to minimize inflammation in his lungs and inhibit the return of his lung disease. His face was worn and a persistent cough kept him from finishing most sentences. But with a spark in his eye, humility spilled forth as he expressed how much he longed to get right with God, his family, and his friends.

Ironically, with no job Jeff had no health insurance. He faced a potentially devastating $100,000 out-of-pocket medical bill. Like Michael's, Jeff's illness was an immune system problem. Yet Jeff's doctors could not define what caused his illness, much less explain his rapid recovery. Jeff believes it was the Good Shepherd's way to bring back one "lost sheep." He remembered this event with humility and a thankful heart:

I'm grateful to God for giving me another chance. I could have easily died, but by His grace and through the prayers of others, I'm in recovery. He's helping me to recover for reasons that I am now on a mission to discover—but I know in a big way it's gonna be about helping others. I gave a lot to the organization I love and lost sight of the most important things in life. I now have three simple goals: to be restored as an even better father and husband than I once was; to get healthy; and to walk with Jesus one day at a time.

I am blessed with compassionate "angels" who prayed for me and now support me in my road to recovery. I also have a new appreciation for my spirituality and compassion as I understand even more deeply the needs of all God's children, whether they are churchgoers or someone sitting in a bar. I am not sure what the future holds but now I know how much people really do care.

The visits, letters, cards and comments on websites from people I knew and loved showed me compassion is always there, to be given and to receive. It is the hand, heart and hope of God that I can now extend to others no matter how desperate their lives may be.

On my twin girls' soccer team Lucy Stancliff runs her five-year-old heart out from one end of the field to the other. Her contagious smile can melt an ogre's heart. She stops to pull up a dandelion, laughs at the boys making weird faces, and kicks the ball hard into the net.

Three years earlier, Lucy fought for her life and eyesight. She had retinoblastoma, or cancer of the eye. She endured multiple surgeries and medical procedures at local and regional hospitals. Her parents, Steve and Amy, each had jobs prior to Lucy's diagnosis and treatment, but faced financial challenges as Amy took leave from her job to be with Lucy. Travel and medical expenses compounded the problem.

Steve taught at a high school and had insurance coverage for his family, but they were financially stretched. Recognizing the Stancliff's challenges, Steve's students adopted Lucy as a Sparrow and raised funds to help offset the medical and living expenses associated with caring for a very sick child.

"With my benefits and pay we were in okay shape, but the emotional lift and extra funds really did help, and Amy was able to spend more time with Lucy. It also meant a lot to the kids at my school," explained Steve. "Adopting Lucy and her cause lifted the school spirit and gave many kids self-esteem boosts. And, for families without the resources we have, I know Sparrow Clubs are critical to their financial survival and emotional healing."

Lucy endured twenty eye surgeries and cancer treatments, including chemotherapy. Today, this Sparrow scores goals, loves chocolate, and laughs at a wink. In the movement of generosity sparked by Jeff Leeland, Lucy's bright future is sealed with the generosity of others.

THE EVOLUTION AND IMPACT
OF AMERICAN HEALTH INSURANCE

To understand the Leeland's dire and perplexing predicament, and those of countless others, it is important to examine the evolution of the health insurance industry in America.

Interestingly, health insurance histories in Canada and Europe follow a similar timeline as the United States, but the present day outcomes are remarkably different for each. Primarily socialized medicine in Canada and Europe and America's largely privatized system account for these differences.

In the late 1800s insurance policies were created for health issues caused by accidents only. Other policies in the form of disability insurance were invented, but limited to individuals or trade groups on an association or narrow regional basis.

A typical program was funded by individuals belonging to labor groups who paid ten cents a month for the right to be diagnosed with an injury or illness that kept them from working.

However, actual medical services were paid for on a fee-for-services basis.

At this same time in Europe, "sickness funds" (similar to disability funds then in the U.S.) were gaining popularity and soon were government-mandated in most countries.

Industries and trades were required to contribute to these funds for employees. In America, however, this required sickness fund payment approach met resistance by owners who felt it an intrusion into managing their own business.

In the early 1900s, Progressive Party members began to push for a national coverage system that would make health insurance compulsory. This movement gained traction with the concept that keeping people healthy would reduce costs for businesses and maintain worker productivity.

At this time there were no real health insurance policies in place. The primary employee benefit was life insurance. The advocates for health insurance proposed that those life insurance premiums could apply to health coverage instead, rendering a more productive citizenry. The life insurance industry fought this, believing that profits would tumble.

The First World War was a catalyst for significant social and economic change in the U.S. With "The Great War" came an anti-German sentiment that led Americans to dislike the ideas of socialized insurance coverage. The rise of Russia's Bolshevism further heightened concerns of socialism in the United States.

Concurrently, rampant industrialization and modernization of industries led to growth in health care technologies and treatments such as vaccines for tuberculosis, heart catheters, insulin discovery, and significant improvements in anesthesia for surgery. This leap in medical science led to higher health care fees. Soon the average expense for a hospital stay in America cost up to half the average annual salary.

To provide equitable treatment options and become more profitable, in the late 1920s Baylor Hospital in Texas created what many consider the first modern health insurance plan. This Blue Cross plan allowed for a local school district teacher to receive up to twenty days of hospital care a year in exchange for fifty cents a month, if at least 75 percent of the teachers in the district were enrolled in the plan. The first person to capitalize on the policy was a teacher who broke her ankle in December of 1929.

The plan was adopted by hospitals throughout the country, and by 1938, almost three million people belonged to various regional Blue Cross plans. Shortly thereafter, Henry Kaiser created health care plans for his industrial businesses throughout California. The success of his program, both in profitability for Kaiser and timely health care for his employees, led to the Kaiser Permanente plan offered to the public in 1945.

The Blue Shield plans were originally formed in the 1930s by Northwest railroad and lumber workers and supported by non-hospital employed physicians. The programs were regional non-profit tools designed to help employees. Premiums were the same for all participants, regardless of health status or age. These plans were embraced by hospitals that preferred a more predictable base of paying patients. Patients without insurance who needed "charity care" were costly to them.

By 1950, over twenty million people belonged to Blue Cross and Blue Shield (the "Blues") programs, leading many to believe that a national health care system like those of most European countries was unnecessary.

With the success of the Blues, commercial insurance providers who had previously stayed away from health policies moved into the market. They competed with the Blues by offering healthier customers lower rates. The Blues used a community-pricing model that offered all members of a geographic or occupational community the same premium for coverage, regardless of individual health status.

Commercial companies created a pricing structure based on an experience rating, meaning healthier clients paid lower premiums. Actuary tables became the foundation for this pricing model, enabling insurers to calculate needed premiums to offset likely coverage expenses.

From this sprang the notion not to cover preexisting conditions to minimize potential expenses, while providing competitively priced policies. Other impacts included the need for physicals prior to obtaining coverage and the growth of individual versus group policies.

At the same time significant advancements in medical care were again taking place. Heart-lung machines, organ transplants, ultrasound technologies, and new vaccinations for deadly diseases, including polio, were created during the 1950s and 1960s.

With these developments and the golden years for unionized industries across America came the demand for ubiquitous health insurance policies. Commercial insurance companies largely met this demand. Less than 10 percent of the population had health insurance in 1940 while almost 70 percent of the nation had insurance in 1960.

Commercial insurance companies had found a profitable product in health insurance. Their market share grew steadily against the Blues throughout the 1950s and 1960s. Additionally, health insurance seemed to directly impact the demand for health care. As reported by Professor Melissa Thomasson in a 2004 report in *Explorations in Economic History*, in 1958:

> *Overall mean total medical expenses totaled $559 annually for families with an individual contract through a commercial insurance company, compared to $314 in spending on medical care by uninsured households.*

This meant that the medical care industry would grow simply based on the power of insurance.

In the early 1960s health insurance covered only 7 percent of medical bills among seniors. Additionally, waves of war generation retirees were no longer eligible for employer-based health insurance. This lack of coverage was a cause of concern for many as the population of older Americans grew and the perceived need to provide health care for seniors expanded.

Medicare and Medicaid was the outcome of this concern. In 1965, President Lyndon Johnson, as part of his Great Society legislative agenda, signed Medicare and Medicaid into law. These two government-based programs assured seniors of fair health care essentially through government funding.

Seniors immediately capitalized on this new coverage. Health care demand among this group previously unable to pay for services was replaced by a sharp increase in services and an increase in pricing.

Medical practitioners also realized that with government sponsorship health care pricing could increase, despite the intent of the legislation to control how much doctors, hospitals, and others could charge. Insurance companies increased their premiums as well to compete with rising health care costs. Ultimately insurance and health care costs skyrocketed in the 1970s and 1980s with supply and demand effects on pricing and macroeconomic inflation.

To control costs and maximize profits, insurance companies focused on reshaping and controlling the health care market. Health Maintenance Organizations (HMOs) and managed care programs gained a strong presence in the 1970s and 1980s.

Following Kaiser Permanente's model of comprehensive health care for a fixed monthly fee, legislation to slow down the upwardly spiraling costs led to the exponential growth of HMOs.

Grants, loans, and other government incentives, combined with insurers realizing they could further define benefits, resulted in an increase of HMOs from six million participants in 1975 to twenty-six million in 1986.

Alongside individuals motivated by employers seeking less expensive insurance options, doctors were strongly encouraged by insurance companies to join HMOs as plan providers. Doctors in managed care programs were assured via sheer number of participants in the plan, (who were required to go to a plan doctor) a steady flow of clients in exchange for reduced service bills.

Today, virtually all other Western industrialized nations have some form of socialized medicine in place. The United Kingdom, Canada, Germany, Sweden, and France each provide some form of health care protection for its citizenry that does not require commercial insurance. These countries also have private health care services for the patients who prefer alternate options to a government plan.

By the mid-1990s, during which insurance companies lost billions in investments from the savings and loan crisis of the early to mid-1980s, approximately 75 percent of all insured persons belonged to a managed care program. Doctors, hospitals, and patients were displaced as sole health care decision-makers when the insurance companies gained control of health care service delivery via mandates for reduced medical costs. Plan administrators were now defining acceptable care standards with a bottom line of cost-effective treatment. In *One Nation Uninsured*, Jill Quadagno wrote:

> *Physicians were pressured*
> *to spend less time with*
> *each individual patient, to*

use fewer specialists, and to order fewer tests and procedures. When physicians challenged the decisions, statisticians pulled out their spreadsheets to demonstrate how the doctors' choice of treatment deviated from the norm. Some HMOs tethered physicians' incomes to patient treatment decisions. Physicians who kept costs under control were rewarded with incentive pay or bonuses as high as $150,000 a year, while those who failed to do so were threatened with "delisting." According to one national survey, over 70 percent of managed care plans used some type of physician profiling.

Within this system Michael Leeland's fate floundered, along with countless others. Since this very low point in the evolution of America's health insurance industry, the situation has improved. Still, most find insurance companies driving too many decisions and view the cost of insurance as prohibitively high.

Premiums have climbed at a rate over four times that of other costs of living. According to a September 2009 article in *USA Today*, from 1999 to 2009 family health insurance premiums rose 131 percent versus 28 percent for the general rate of inflation.

With the passage of the Affordable Care Act in 2010, children under nineteen years of age—today's Michael Leelands—are no longer excluded from coverage for preexisting conditions. This rule applies whether or not a child's health problem or disability was discovered or treated before coverage was applied for.

The insurance industry, individual states, and citizen groups filed lawsuits and have taken steps to challenge the program's constitutionality. These include the five for-profit companies that control 39 percent of the commercial Medicare and Medicaid health insurance market. This group created a consortium to fight the bill. The Supreme Court ultimately ruled that the Affordable Care Act was constitutional.

DENNIS GUTHRIE

Devotion

The way you get meaning into your life is to devote yourself to loving others, devote yourself to your community around you, and devote yourself to creating something that gives you purpose and meaning.

—MITCH ALBOM

The "pyschs" say I am still trying to save those that I couldn't. I don't know why I do it, but as long as someone needs help I will keep going.

—DENNIS GUTHRIE

E nemy soldiers targeted by an 82mm mortar do not hear much when it is launched. The light, highly portable explosive was the weapon of choice for the North Vietnamese Army and Vietcong guerillas to attack American soldiers during the war that raged across Southeast Asia in the 1960s and 1970s. Its noise, when heard from a distance, is a hollow *thoomp* that sounds a bit like a cardboard tube being struck with a mallet.

After the distant *thoomp* comes the waiting. With the extreme arc of its trajectory, an incoming mortar round possesses the perverse quality of exploding quickly—say three to five seconds—when it overshoots your position or hangs in the atmosphere for an eternity if it is going to strike close by. Men who have suffered repeated bombardments quickly learn to count the seconds between the time the initial detonation is heard until the explosion.

A growing interval means the enemy is "walking them in"—adjusting the mortar to drop the aerial bombs closer and closer until on target. A count of five or six might mean a concussion inside your troop's post perimeter; seven means someone died a few foxholes over. A count of eight, nine, ten and the knowledge of an impending, skull-shattering blast of jagged shrapnel and gobs of burning phosphorous in the surrounding air becomes a shrieking certainty.

Some scream, some pray, and some die quietly, but for those who survive, a primitive part of the brain remains forever coiled and ready to snap into a mad scramble for cover at any faint signal of hostile fire. If you were a member of the American armed forces in Vietnam in 1969, this reaction was a matter of survival. Like twenty-year-old Dennis Guthrie of Portland, Oregon, if you were a medic with Company B of the First Battalion of the Seventh Calvary of the U.S. Army, it was necessary not only to survive, but to tend to those ripped and burned and torn by the shells.

Dennis Guthrie's path to war was not unusual. Only eighteen months earlier he was a college student, studying to become a science teacher. With no plans to enter the military, he imagined himself safe from the war by an education deferment, until a summer job between semesters disqualified him and he received a letter from his local draft board. "Greetings from the President of the United States" the letter began, and went on to inform him that "a board composed of your neighbors" found him suitable for military service. He was ordered to prepare for induction into one of the four branches of service.

Guthrie enlisted before the draft. During basic training he excelled at advanced infantry tactics and received one of the highest scores on record for a course in leadership preparation. After basic, he volunteered for airborne training, where he performed well enough to receive a coveted invitation to join the Green Berets. Dennis shined during this training and high marks earned him his Beret as a medic-in-training in the elite unit. Guthrie was in the top of his class in physical conditioning and passed the oral and hands-on skills tests. When he failed the written exam by a few points due to dyslexia, he decided to forgo another year of medic school and volunteered again, this time for war.

Within weeks Guthrie was dropped into firefights first as a ground medic and then from evacuation helicopters. He spiraled down through pell-mell machine gun fire to snatch critically wounded American soldiers out of the fray. He earned his first decoration, a Bronze Star, when he army-crawled through a muddy field to drag a man to safety. He also earned the Air Medal for Heroism when he hung from a hovering chopper under intense enemy fire to hoist a wounded man aboard.

But it was his actions on August 12, 1969, that earned him a spot among the most decorated enlisted men in history. The official narrative on Guthrie's Silver Star Award reads:

> [When] a numerically superior enemy force initiated a rocket and recoilless rifle attack, coupled with a ground attack on his company's position, Specialist Guthrie immediately deployed to the section most severely hit and pulled six comrades from two destroyed bunkers. Although constantly under enemy fire, Specialist Five Guthrie crawled from position to position while throwing grenades and laying down suppressive fire upon the enemy. After tending to the wounded, he withdrew to the center of the perimeter and returned with reinforcements to fill the gaps in the defense.

Over forty years later, Guthrie still brushes his accomplishments aside. "I can't explain why I did what I did and how and why others do what they do. Don't make me out to be a hero. I was only doing what I was supposed to do." With a reddening face, burning eyes, and tight jaw he continued. "I don't care who you are or how you try to philosophize about war; whether you are Jesus or Gandhi, all of the bullshit goes right out the window. All you are trying to do is survive." So it was on the night of August 12, in Vietnam's Tay Ninh province.

Dennis snapped awake at the distant thump. Listening, counting and sprinting from his tent, he hit the bunker several yards from the canvas door at the count of seven and watched the bunker two down from his explode, the screams of soldiers shredded by 82mm shrapnel piercing the sticky night air. The communication radios crackled with shouts that "Charlie"— the enemy—was coming fast and hard.

The enemy was inside the line, less than one hundred yards from Dennis' position. Mortar puffs followed deafening explosions that gave the enemy cover and took American lives as the rifle-bearing Vietcong crept out of the trees like a deadly fog. Only muzzle flashes and mortar blasts were visible in the pitch black, but Dennis and his comrades knew they were outnumbered. Bombs, machine-gun fire, and wails of the injured raged as gunpowder and dying men burned.

In a six-bunker row the four hard to Dennis' side were under full attack. Dennis' bunker, with two men dead, was next in line to fall. He grabbed one dead man's M-16 and unleashed a barrage of fury on enemy lines, determined that this night wouldn't be his last. His rapid fire superheated the barrel until it bent, broken down.

He grabbed the other dead man's gun, careful this time with calculated shots to save that weapon and buy some time. Heaving dozens of grenades and pumping bullets into the darkness, Dennis reached into the ammo can one more time and came up empty—eighty hand grenades and hundreds of bullets later. With one .45-caliber handgun left, Dennis was out of any real firepower options.

A remaining soldier sat in his bunk waiting to die: head down, knees pulled close, frozen in fear. Dennis left the bunker to rescue wounded soldiers, then returned. He horse-collared the petrified soldier, pulled his face in close to his and ordered the man to get his shit together or they both would die. The soldier snapped to and provided cover fire for Dennis as he moved from one to the next, pulling soldiers back from the fray.

With one hand harboring the wounded and the other wielding his 45, Dennis battled for time and the lives of men. After an hour, Dennis hurried around the bunkers below short ridgelines to a distant command post. He requested help, crawled back to his position, and was soon aided by reinforcements that kept the enemy at bay long enough for him to survive. As dawn arrived, the faceless enemy vanished into the jungle and Dennis tended to the wounded.

The Silver Star is the third highest military award medal presented to soldiers. Nearly three million men and women have served in the military and fewer than 150,000 Silver Stars were presented since the medal's inception in 1932. Given to soldiers who exhibit "gallantry in action" against enemy forces, this medal is considered the highest possible honor for those not within the military command hierarchy.

Silver Stars are typically awarded to infantryman carrying heavy firepower or to ace pilots with five or more kills. Dennis had only his .45-caliber handgun and displaced emotions. "You build up a wall and stop letting scared be a part of your life after the first few weeks," explained Dennis. "You have to in order to survive and not deal with the emotions. The whole scene is unreal."

Fighting to survive impacts each soldier differently but the emotional detachment is universal. "As a helicopter medic, one minute you are playing cards and drinking a beer at a support base and the next you are onboard heading into what you know will be a bloody mess. Thoughts and feelings go away as your survival senses just take over. There is no other choice," shared Dennis.

"The 'psychs' tell me this goes back to evolutionary fight-or-flight instincts that come from the base of your brain, your most primal control area. In order to be hyper-vigilant, the sense of smell, the intuition of strange movement around you, and your awareness of peculiar noises near and far—all of these things kick in and you are in absolute focus mode simply to survive."

"You know how to make a sword, right?" Dennis asked, breathing shallow as he answered his own question. "You stick the iron into burning fire, get it super hot and you take it out and pound on it and shape it into something basic." His focus narrowed as he channeled memories from the battlefront.

"Then you stick it back in the fire, and get it red hot again and then you take it out and pound on it to get it sharper. Then you stick it back in the fire to make it stronger and you take it out and keep hammering and hammering at it. That is like being in war. You get stronger or you die."

Combat soldiers learn how to shut their emotions off because war is too painful if they don't. "Emotion is sent away," continued Dennis. "Survival starts with reactionary instincts hardened from being in battle. From there you have to adapt to each situation. Even still, there are no guarantees, no absolutes. The most aware and focused, the most emotionally removed and most fanatically adapted soldier can die in an instant from just plain bad luck."

During his tours, Dennis saved countless lives and gave what comfort he could to others as the last light left their eyes.

Some of his most selfless efforts to help the wounded and maimed would come years later.

Nearly sixty thousand soldiers died in Vietnam. (See article page 165.) Survivors weathered over ten times more direct combat than those from prior wars. War zone hospitals and troop transport helicopters ferried the same wounded warriors to and from battle in an exhaustive, man-eating cycle. Why some die and others don't is a mystery too big for most.

"One guy just gets shot in the shoulder, clean through, and needs a simple bandage, but then he dies," recalled Dennis. "Another has both legs blasted off, one arm no longer there, and I am trying to get an IV in his only good appendage, and he just wants to tell me dirty jokes as we are flying out of the battle. Each person reacts differently to the situation; some die, some live, all go home different than they came."

Many of those who came home never left the war behind. The healing process was slow or not at all, especially when a hoped-for hug of recognition never came. Jeff Casserly served with the Third Marine Division providing support to frontline soldiers from his post in North Da Nang, Vietnam. "I wasn't back a week and I was ready to leave," shared Jeff. "It was like someone had dropped me on a different planet. I had zero connection to the people around me. It was as if we were not speaking the same language. If the people, the environment, had just been welcoming, just listened, it would have made a world of difference."

World War II veterans paraded down Main Streets big and small as the conquerors of evil. Soldiers who returned from the Korean War earned praise as victors over a known communist enemy. The reception given to Vietnam soldiers was nothing of the sort. "Vietnam vets did not need to be considered heroes, but we should not have been disregarded or disliked. America did not embrace us. In fact, there was shame," said Jeff. "Not only did the American public not understand what we went through, they did not understand why we were at war in the first place."

Perhaps it was live footage from the war piped into America's living rooms, or conflicted sentiments swept into Washington by the hippy movement. The public's distaste for the war was visceral and for this reason, peace was not at home for returning veterans, the most tragic irony of all. "The threat of communism expanding did not make a lot of sense to folks—there was no real known enemy—and based on the body counts broadcast every night there were young men seen as dying for no real cause," explained Jeff.

Returning veterans were cast away without cover. A lot of people died emotionally. A lot had only time and no other tools to heal. They were required to fix themselves. Many veterans suffered emotional challenges, mental illness, turned to substance abuse, or worse.

"So many just opted out instead of existing. Whether it was drugs, suicide, violence, or just emotionally removed, we were all crippled," Jeff continued. But strengths sometimes won out. "For many others and me, over time we became stronger and did not run away. I began to trust in my own abilities. But, I don't think a lifetime would clear all the issues. In one form or another you become a junkie."

Post-Traumatic Stress Disorder (PTSD) and other trauma-related psychoses manifest differently for each person who endures the hell of war. Some wrestle with severe cases while others don't. While distinguished officers and Privates First Class have jobs that pay a living wage or own companies that earn millions, others attend Alcoholics Anonymous meetings or find the grace of God in houses of refuge. Many march up and down the streets at night waiting for daylight. Others take innocent lives, or their own. Dennis still fights his demons since returning to Oregon. "You have to learn how to survive the surviving," said Dennis.

PTSD was not officially recognized as a combat-related injury or disability by the U.S. government until nearly ten years after the last American troops returned home from Vietnam. (See article page 167) Prior to the 1980s these "side effects" of war were ignored, hidden, and denied by men and women who felt they were alone in their suffering. The nightmares, depression, suicide, and difficulty adjusting now understood as insidious war-inflicted injuries were then dismissed as personal failings or character flaws.

Just a couple weeks after returning to the States, Dennis stood on the front lawn of his parents' home in Portland. A car cruised down the quaint neighborhood street as Dennis talked quietly with his mother. The car backfired. Dennis went into action. "I tackled my mom and drove her into the ground in order for her to not get shot, and dove into the hedge along my house to take cover. It all came back. The emotions that got in the way of staying alive in Vietnam got buried again in that instant," he said.

Years after returning from Vietnam, Dennis and his wife went to watch the movie *Saving Private Ryan*. They sat in the very back of the theater, where you can survey all that happens in front of you. The booming surround sound shook the theater in the opening scene of soldiers hitting the beach. "I kicked into survival mode. I began giving orders to imaginary soldiers," said Dennis. "My wife's tapping on my leg and whispers that we were just watching a movie brought me back to the present."

"It has been explained to me like this. Most decisions in day-to-day life are made via a process that resembles a triangle," shared Dennis. "The left base angle is an action or event in your environment. The right base angle is a reaction to that event. The peak point represents the thought."

Common events and scenes like a group of people standing on the corner when you go for a walk, the smell of something burning, or a car backfiring start the reaction process. "A 'normal' person registers the input on the lower left point of the triangle and then it climbs up that side of the triangle to your thoughts. You figure out what these actions might mean to you and then your thoughts run down the right side to the reaction. You behave normally as you figure out how to address the issue in a rationale manner," said Dennis.

The scars of war change how Dennis reacts to everyday life. "Regular processing of information does not apply," continued Dennis. "You go straight along the base of the triangle from action to reaction. There is no thought. That is why I threw my mom to the ground and jumped into the bushes."

PTSD affects nearly half a million former fighters, including Dennis. It is the leading health care issue among veterans who were engaged in violent military action. It plagues

Vietnam veterans and more recent veterans as well. Of the two hundred thousand Iraq and Afghanistan veterans who suffer from PTSD, only 20 percent have asked for help. The suicide rate among active duty forces is the highest it has ever been, and is responsible for 15 percent of all casualties. Every eighty minutes a U.S. war veteran attempts suicide; every day one actually succeeds.

There is a clear correlation between modern warfare and the growing number of PTSD victims. Long deployments, excessive combat trauma, and repeated tours are suspected causes. Jeff Casserly sees a positive shift in caregiver attitudes and treatment. "I think it is different now. Given the number of Gulf War vets coming back from multiple tours of duty, it better be and has to be. Today, veterans are honored and taken care of, which is good and critical. They may be suffering more than we did."

In his first twenty years after escaping Vietnam, Dennis could not settle down. He found work as a truck driver and construction worker and fell in and out of relationships. Getting too emotionally attached meant losing control and facing his shell shock. Despite the emotional hurdles, Dennis fell in love with an old girlfriend and got married. He raised a family, felt vindicated by a government finally recognizing the mental trauma among veterans, and volunteered for and was elected to several posts with the Veterans of Foreign Wars (VFW).

Dennis was elected the Redmond, Oregon local post commander for four terms and the VFW regional commander for two terms. He also served on the board of the Central Oregon Veterans Council, which provides state legislatures advice on veterans' issues. In these positions, Dennis testified on behalf of veterans to various government boards and committees.

Dennis sits quietly over a cup of coffee in a local restaurant when he spies a man about his age wearing a familiar hat. He knows it is one that only a veteran would wear. He politely approaches the man and they strike up a brief conversation about their respective service. The bond is palpable and tender at the surface, and Dennis' desire to engage is reflected in the appreciative glow of the stranger's eyes.

By simply engaging the man, Dennis heals two souls. He explained why he does this wherever he goes: "The pyschs say I am still trying to save those that I couldn't. Only 1 percent of the population in this country has ever served in the military, and fewer than that has seen active war duty. With no disrespect, how can this other 99 percent relate to battle-worn veterans? I don't know why I do it, but as long as someone needs help I will keep going."

Dennis used this mantra when he was elected VFW Surgeon General and served a two-year term from 2009 to 2010. With over two million active members across ten thousand posts around the world, VFW is the leading advocacy group for returning U.S. soldiers. In 2008, the VFW won a long-fought victory with the authorization of an updated G.I. Bill. The bill granted stronger educational benefits to America's active-duty service members and members of the National Guard and Reserves fighting in Iraq and Afghanistan.

As a top national post in the VFW, the Surgeon General communicates veterans' concerns to the Veterans Administration and Congress. To gain an accurate representation of veteran's concerns, Dennis personally surveyed existing facilities and veteran's services across the country. (See article page 168.)

Over a ten week period, Dennis traveled through twelve states and covered ten thousand miles to know and *feel* the medical and social challenges facing veterans. He investigated over twenty hospitals and medical clinics and visited twenty-five VFW meeting facilities. For months he created reports and gave presentations to veteran organizations and government branches to voice his concerns about modern treatment options. He funded the trip from his own pocket and retirement fund. Dennis summarized his end-of-term report to the VA and VFW:

I have seen great innovations, new ideas, and a great desire and passion to help our veterans of all ages and at all levels. I believe we need to emphasize the positive and build on that. But at the same time we need to be open to the concerns and criticisms of the programs so that we can make them better; especially in those cases where veterans feel they have been overlooked. When you are in pain or worried about cancer, time goes by very slowly. We also know that when you are involved in the largest health care system in the world there will be problems. It is how we face these challenges and resolve the problems that we will be judged on in the future.

To honor Vietnam veterans years after the war ended, the Vietnam Veterans Memorial was built. There are two sections of the Vietnam Memorial Wall, each measuring 246-feet-long. It is a quiet sentinel near the Lincoln Memorial in Washington D.C. with the name of every known soldier who died in Vietnam etched into its coal-black marble.

For those who are unable to make it to our nation's capital but still wish to experience this memorial, a replica was built. Nearly 80 percent of the official wall's size, the "Moving Wall" now tours the country. From Atlanta, Georgia, to Portland, Oregon, the wall travels the U.S in unassembled panels and is set up by teams of locals to honor this largely forgotten group of veterans.

In 2010, Dennis and Jeff led the effort to bring the Moving Wall to Redmond, Oregon. The event featured speakers, helicopters and military vehicle displays, motorcycle escorts of the wall en route to and out of Redmond, and memorials for local soldiers. Veterans, their families, and curious community members were touched.

A couple in their eighties knelt and placed a vase of flowers at the base of the memorial; their tears spilled into the jar. A woman in her sixties trembled as her finger traced an etching. Two young men stood in an open embrace and scanned the sea of names. Children played in a nearby ball field with an innocence far removed from war.

I came to the memorial with my son. As I touched the wall my stomach fell when I locked on the names of two boys from my childhood neighborhood: Jimmy Nicholson and Billy Roddick.

Jimmy and Billy lived on a quiet, dead-end street surrounded by orange groves at the base of ten-thousand-foot mountains. This neighborhood hosted backyard swim parties, birthdays, anniversaries, weddings and Dodger games on the AM radio under a covered patio. But this idyllic picture of American pastime was shattered in a period of less than six months. Jimmy, the big brother of my best friend who lived next door, and Billy whose parents owned the house with the pool, were killed in Vietnam.

On the wall they were listed as James Alexander Nicholson and William Henry Roddick, but everyone called them Jimmy and Billy; generally people call you by a name that ends in "y" when you are a kid. It was hard to call them anything else. They both died in 1969, at twenty years old, with parents at home, waiting. They were not alone in the group of soldiers too young to die. Almost twenty-five thousand of those killed in Vietnam were twenty years old or younger. The pain I felt for them at the wall was deeper than I had ever experienced. I hugged my son and told him I loved him.

At the wall ceremony, Dennis gave a passionate speech about the challenges those who return from war continue to face, and scars that don't completely heal. War takes no survivors and all who come away are the walking wounded. Dennis is one who works tirelessly to ensure they are well cared for.

With thousands of Vietnam War veterans still alive and troops coming home from Iraq and Afghanistan every day, the work goes on. Dennis still lobbies dignitaries and the general public to provide effective treatment for returning soldiers. "Dennis is a war hero. And his pain runs very deep," said Jeff. The spectrum of health for returning veterans is vast.

How they handle the trauma of war can look like assuming the fetal position or attacking life with a vengeance.

"Dennis is very outspoken, even loud, about the injustices he sees," Jeff continued. "He can rub you the wrong way but then you realize this is his way of dealing with the scars of war." Dennis refuses to take a quiet backseat about his causes. "At least now his emotions are felt rather than repressed as he passionately serves our veterans. This is a sign that, finally, some of us are healing," said Jeff.

Every Friday night in Redmond, war veterans gather to have a drink and a moment or two with old friends. They pass through the solid wooden doors of an old but lovingly cared-for building that sits just east of the railroad tracks in the middle of a dirt parking lot. Some are missing teeth, others limbs, most a piece of their heart, and all some degree of innocence. Old timers and younger soldiers gather around memories and beers. This VFW post is like hundreds across the country. Quiet heroes toast to days gone by and better ones to come.

On Saturdays you can find the same group together again. Veterans' sons and granddaughters, nieces and nephews, or just family friends round up for a pellet gun target competition or a raffle to support their favorite cause. The air is light, far removed from the caustic smoke of a battlefield. Their good-natured ribbing and cheers for the winner fill the hall. This is why they gather. There are other reasons, but you catch them only if you look and listen closely. Devotion silently runs from one heart to another and solace is never loud.

THE VIETNAM WAR
IN ASIA AND AMERICA

The Vietnam War was fought from August 1964 to April 1975. It began when a U.S. battleship was hit by artillery fire off the coast of South Vietnam, and ended when the South Vietnamese city of Saigon fell to the North Vietnamese. The motivation behind U.S. involvement was stopping the spread of communism.

North Vietnam was a communist country that had invaded the more democratic South Vietnam to forcibly unite the two countries. Countries like China and Cambodia backed North Vietnam while South Vietnam became allied with the United States, France, South Korea, Australia, and Great Britain.

While statistics do not accurately reflect the essence of war, they are important to understand the magnitude of Vietnam. It was the longest war in America's history, although war was never officially declared. More than 58,000 American soldiers were killed and over 300,000 were injured. An es-

timated three million people lost their lives. The day-to-day intensity of the war was far greater than any prior conflict. The average infantryman saw approximately two hundred forty days a year of combat in Vietnam versus ten days a year during World War II.

This was largely from the use of helicopters that shuttled soldiers into and out of violent action. There were over half a million medical evacuation helicopter missions in Vietnam—a number that does not include separate helicopter combat missions.

Vietnam was the first war televised for the world to see. While footage was not as sophisticated as that of modern embedded reporters, the general public was able to see on nightly news the impact of war on soldiers and civilians. Ninety-three percent of all households had television sets during the mid-1960s.

The news reporting on the war, while gruesome, was initially supportive of U.S. efforts to contain communism. However, in 1968 the sentiment shifted. The bloody Tet Offensive, when North Vietnamese soldiers destroyed countless South Vietnam villages, was regarded as excessively violent. This led reporters to editorialize that the U.S. could not win a war against this enemy.

Ironically, the Tet Offensive was reported as a victory for the North even though the battle to contain communism was demoralizing and destructive to Vietcong troops. According to Dennis Guthrie, they threw everything they had at the U.S. but did not succeed. This event and others heightened negativity and suspicion with nightly stories of the Mai Lai massacre, where U.S. soldiers killed 350 civilians.

As many lost hope for a good outcome, others stood fast with the Nixon administration's efforts. College and university students sparked anti-war campaigns while Main Street Americans waved flags in support of the troops. Anti-war activists catalyzed a movement that divided the country and sought our military's complete withdrawal from Southeast Asia.

Violence erupted throughout the U.S. at Kent State, the Chicago Democratic Convention, and elsewhere, in the heat of the protest. Activists became empowered and brazen with their message. The country was fighting a painful philosophical war at home while young soldiers engaged death in a distant and inhospitable Asian jungle.

The war gave rise to two painfully polarized fronts. One side felt it imperative to fight the spread of communism. The other considered the war fundamentally unjust. Some soldiers followed orders and others followed convictions, but many men paid in blood for both ideologies. Those who survived the muddy hell now seek peace of mind on the streets of America.

POST-TRAUMATIC STRESS DISORDER
AND SUICIDE

More than thirteen million people in the United States today suffer from Post-Traumatic Stress Disorder (PTSD). Of that number, two million are war veterans. PTSD is a psychological injury caused by exposure to extreme trauma.

From rape to assault, car accidents to grenade attacks, victims of single or multiple violent events can suffer irreparable damage to their nervous system and behavior patterns.

According to nonprofit resource Helpguide:

Following a traumatic event, almost everyone experiences at least some of the symptoms of PTSD. When your sense of safety and trust are shattered, it's normal to feel crazy, disconnected, or numb. It's very common to have bad dreams, feel fearful or numb, and find it difficult to stop thinking about what happened. These are normal reactions to abnormal events.

After a traumatic experience, the mind and body are in shock. As victims process their emotions and make sense of what happened, most return from that state of shock. With PTSD, victims remain in shock. PTSD sufferers can be hyper-nervous, ultra-isolated, and even violent as the injury forces them to relive the traumatic experience.

There are myriad symptoms associated with PTSD, including flashbacks to the event, nightmares, numbing, sleep deprivation, agitation and excitability. While there are threads of behavioral similarities among PTSD victims ,there is no standard diagnostic tool.

PTSD impacts the lives of veterans in tragic ways. Veterans account for approximately 30 percent of suicides in the nation. If you are a veteran you are twice as likely to attempt suicide than if you are not. From homelessness to substance abuse, murder to suicide, the ravages of war continue long after the days and nights of survival in a war zone.

VETERANS HEALTH ADMINISTRATION

There are approximately 22 million veterans in the U.S. today. The Veterans Health Administration provides care for them as the single largest health care provider in the U.S., with over 170 medical center hospitals, 350 outpatient clinics, and 126 nursing homes.

The history of the Veterans Affairs health system is older than our country. It began when the pilgrims of Plymouth Colony passed a law for the community to support disabled soldiers who fought against the Peqout Indians.

Both the Revolutionary War and Civil War prompted legislation requiring the federal government to provide health benefits to soldiers returning from war, primarily in the form of care homes. The First World War instituted more change in the system for injured veterans to obtain health insurance and vocational training.

The years between World War II and the Vietnam War saw the greatest improvements in services. These came on the heels of a near systemic failure caused by shortcomings in VA facilities across the nation. With an aging veterans population and an influx of new ones from Vietnam, the hospital-based system was woefully inadequate for soldiers needing outpatient or periodic assistance.

The lack of facilities displaced appropriate health care for hundreds of thousands of veterans, unless they were admitted to the VA hospital. Not to mention the wasteful bureaucratic layers of the Veterans Affairs office that oversaw the VHA. Deserving veteran patients were left with a system mired in deficiency.

In the mid-1990s an outsider with decades of private medical care experience became the head of the VHA and turned it around. Dr. Kenneth Kizer created a program of multi-faceted comprehensive care practices governed on a regional basis.

The Veterans Integrated Service Network (VISN) installed veteran healthcare practices on a community level to provide inpatient, outpatient, mental health, and rehabilitation services to veterans in non-institutional settings and facilities. This reduced demand on hospitals, dropped expenses for health care services, and encouraged proactive care for veterans.

Dr. Kizer was forced to retire within a few years of his appointment, a victim to the politics of the time. However, the groundwork was laid for a successful program. A powerful and streamlined database of veterans' health information was developed and successfully implemented.

For the past eleven years, the VHA performance scores remain exceptional from surveys by veteran patients. Veterans now express more satisfaction with their health care than private sector patients.

BRIANNA MERCADO

Resilience

Although the world is full of suffering, it is also full of the overcoming of it. When we do the best that we can, we never know what miracle is wrought in our life, or in the life of another.
                                                                    —HELEN KELLER

I think Brianna's main goal in life is to prove to everyone, every day, that the power of love is everything.
                                                                    —SABRINA MERCADO

An easy breeze cools Camp Okizu, a five-hundred-acre adventure retreat nestled in California's Feather River watershed. Winds spill down this high Sierra canyon into the Sacramento Valley. The sky above shines with a million stars floating beyond granite peaks. A couple hours before the stars came out, kids ran, fished, super-soaked each other, shrieked with joy, and took deep pure breaths in the peace of this wild place.

Now a warm campfire glows as campers from six to seventeen years old finish their week-long adventure. It is almost time to say goodbye, but the week's closing ceremony—

known as "Inspiration"—provides one more chance to laugh into the fading night, and reflect on a week of just plain fun.

Seven days earlier parents said goodbye as their children boarded a bus to the mountains. Pine cabins, a large bright dining hall with a vista deck, a medical station and an activities room, trails and creeks, kayaking and swimming, running and jumping characterize Camp Okizu. Boys and girls from different places make lifelong friends and sunshine and laughter temporarily replace what life is like back home.

The campers and counselors gather around the stage for the closing ceremony. The eight-year-old boys perform a skit about fishing in a camp lake, making fun of their favorite counselor's instructions to land the fish by keeping the hook out of your ear. The twelve-year-old girls sing a newly-composed song about snoring in their cabin as a way to keep ornery bears and boys at bay.

Fourteen-year-old Danny reads a poem he wrote, expressing all the love and care he felt here at a time it was sorely needed. And fifteen-year-old Becky takes the stage with a humble request for counselors and fellow campers not to forget her. Before turning in for the night and the next day's long ride home, kids on stage share what matters most to them with their new friends and counselors.

Camp Okizu is a place of refuge for children with cancer. For thirty-one years kids have come here to put aside hospital visits, hopelessness, and the strain of being different from their classmates. Bald heads are no big deal. Afternoon naps are a certainty. Living fully in the moment replaces wondering what the future holds.

"It's a lot harder now than it used to be," shared camp cofounder and angel on earth, John Bell. When the camp first started, children's oncology protocols were far less sophisticated and successful.

"At the time we started Camp Okizu roughly half of the children with cancer died. Today, it is down to about 20 to 25 percent and getting better. We now have a reason to expect every child to survive and when some don't make it we are crushed." With tears welling, John recalled his time at various camps over the years, including one particularly hard one. "Within weeks of her request that night, Becky died. She was wearing her camp T-shirt when she passed away."

About half of the volunteer counselors at Camp Okizu—a Sioux word meaning "to come together as one"—are cancer survivors or siblings of cancer fighters. They too spent time in hospitals, away from school, being different. Nicknames like LuLu, Beta, and Topeka replace counselor's actual names as one reflection of the camp's lightheartedness and intent to keep the distraction of "real" life away.

Other volunteers, like Amber—an oncology nurse who provides medical care at the camp—are available to help campers who cannot take breaks from their cancer treatments. "It lifts my spirit," Amber spoke, as we surveyed a colorful meadow while campers drenched their counselors with pails of water. "And I can tell you with complete certainty that it lifts their spirits and is irreplaceably important in their healing."

Most volunteers return summer after summer to strengthen and embolden others. They found their Camp Oziku experience a springboard into a lifetime of giving. Tiffany Chang, who first found Camp Okizu as a teenage counselor, is now a pediatric oncologist and recommends the camp to her patients. Brianna Mercado, aka "Topeka" was changed by it as well. "Camp Okizu is a magical place, and I don't know where I would be without it," said Brianna.

A few years earlier in the early fall of 2005, Brianna swam toward the water polo ball with all of her fifteen-year-old might. She cradled it in her arms, treaded water in the mysterious way only strong polo players can, raised the ball above her head, and pumped it into the goal. Her teammates swarmed her and high-fived. Brianna was having the time of her life playing water polo, leading her dance class, and just hanging out with friends.

While primping for another ninth-grade day a few weeks later, Brianna felt a lump under her arm. She and her mom went to one doctor, then to play it safe another, who both delivered the good news: it was likely just a calcium deposit that would need to be removed "in the future." For the next few months Brianna didn't lose her stride. Her favorite color was yellow like a daisy in full bloom. Brianna and her twin sister and constant companion Sabrina, shopped, swam, and swirled around.

The lump continued to grow and change color and annoyed Brianna as it got in the way of swimming. A third doctor took one look at it, surgically removed it, and sent it off to the lab for routine diagnosis. A few days later the Mercados got a call that was far from routine. The doctor asked them to come down to his office as soon as possible, where he delivered the results of the lab test: Ewing's Sarcoma. Cancer. With her mother dismayed and questioning the fairness of it all, Brianna absorbed the news, but never asked, "Why me?"

An often fatal form of cancer, Ewing's Sarcoma occurs most frequently in teenagers. Ninety percent of the cases occur with patients between five and twenty years of age. The average age is fifteen. It strikes only two in one million people, and only two hundred new diagnoses a year are made in the United States. The cancerous tumor is often found on the tibia, femur, humerus, or scapula or in the immediate soft tissue. If it metastasizes in the body, the odds of long-term survival are less than 10 percent. There is no genetic predisposition for families to screen for it before it manifests as a lump.

Within twelve hours of the diagnosis Brianna had her first appointment with an oncologist. He explained the need to treat this cancer aggressively to whip it. Within one week, Brianna was wheeled from the operating room with a fresh scar where the tumor once was.

Four rounds of chemotherapy immediately followed surgery, but some cancer cells remained. A second and third surgery led Brianna's doctors to believe they had cut out all of the cancer cells, but with a nagging chance the cancer could still remain in her body. To keep it from resurrecting, she would need radiation and more chemotherapy that could last up to a year.

Chemotherapy kills just enough to get rid of bad cells and leaves just enough good cells to rebuild. That is why hair falls out, the body is riddled with open sores, and energy levels drastically plummet. "Right after her second chemotherapy Brianna was in pretty bad shape," recalled Sabrina. "She was drained and her mouth and throat were filled with sores that made it too painful to do much of anything."

From the time they were born Sabrina and Brianna shared a bed, even after their parents separated and they split their time between both households. Now was no exception. "As we lay in bed, I fed her the only thing she could handle: ice chips. I thought she was sleeping because she was so tired and hurt from the treatment, and her eyes were closed. But she summoned enough strength to quietly whisper, 'Thank you.'"

Deep into her chemotherapy treatments, Brianna's appearance scared people. Perhaps her gaunt face, bald head, and the dark circles beneath her eyes evoked a fear of death. She was not allowed many interactions with friends. Once an energetic teenager leading her swim team and dance groups, Brianna was now a frail young girl who struggled to enjoy a walk in the park.

At times all that remained was that spark faintly aglow, the essence that made her somehow powerfully different. "I spent the year with Brianna helping take care of her at the hospital, at my mom's house and my dad's house, and with schoolwork," shared Sabrina. "While there were times that I felt she was the last person on earth to deserve this, she never did. It was as if she knew there was a greater purpose that would come from her being sick."

Brianna recalled this stage of recovery: "It wasn't until I was diagnosed that I became conscious of how many people are suffering. I will never forget the cries that I heard in the hospital as I walked down the hallway and saw rooms packed full of people of every health problem. I needed a way to inform others about this, to speak on behalf of those that could not. I chose not to hide. I walked around skinny, scarred, and stuck with an IV, but with dignity. I had no hair, no eyelashes, no eyebrows, and not a trace of color in my face. But, I could still smile and I tried to do so with radiance. I had never felt so horrible, and yet so amazing. All I wanted was for the world to realize how many ordinary people overcome extraordinary challenges each and every day."

Thousands of teenagers in the U.S. are diagnosed with cancer each year. (See article page 187.) There are thousands more each year who die from it. Parents, friends, and fellow students are all affected when someone they know and love is forced down this path with only a glimmer of hope. Yet through a forest of impenetrable odds, sometimes the individual gains strength and punches a path out of the dark.

"I fought for my life that year. Fourteen rounds of chemotherapy, twenty-five rounds of radiation, six surgeries, and over forty blood and platelet transfusions," Brianna said. After she spent her sophomore year in this fight, test results revealed her cancer was in full remission and life could go on. "I was cut loose. I was allowed my freedom again. Free to be near germs and throw away my medication chart."

Each child with cancer has a story worth telling, a story that incites wonder about the divine plan and gives deeper meaning to life. So why Brianna in this book, instead of another young hero? An inconspicuous Internet article about a small hometown organization reveals why. (See article page 189.)

Sandlot Hero is a nonprofit organization near San Jose, California. It was developed and is headed by Albert Perkins, whose son Justin lost his fight with cancer in 2008. Justin said, "I want to help people after I am gone." His dad honors this commitment with a platform to salute community members who make a difference. Justin made a difference fighting the stomach cancer that eventually took his life. The Sandlot Hero website tells his story:

> Justin was diagnosed during his junior year of high school, shortly after the last football game of the 2003 season. Perkins faced the initial diagnosis with optimism and determination to overcome his cancer, refusing to allow cancer to dampen his academics as well as his zeal for sports. "[He was] soft spoken, an All-American kid… He was a great football player and was a great kid who loved his teammates," Perkins' former football coach Jeff Mueller said.
>
> During his senior year, Perkins was in charge of conditioning the JV football team. Before undergoing chemotherapy, Perkins promised himself that he would play on the varsity football team as a senior, and he fulfilled this promise, playing in the last three games of the year. "It was a really big deal when he got out [on the field to play], and he got standing ovations," Mueller said.
>
> The inspiration [for Sandlot Hero] originates from Justin, whose resilience and courage in his fight with cancer inspired his community. The Sandlot Hero is someone you know from your community that inspires you. Our goal is to share the stories of the ordinary people who do extraordinary things each and every day.

"There's always going to be a pain in my heart," Albert Perkins said in a 2011 Cupertino Patch article. "But I can smile watching the recipients of the award, knowing they have the same passion my son had, knowing people are remembering my son." Perkins founded the award program with friends Steven Young and John Loiacono.

"This award is meant to inspire kids to do things that last beyond their lifetime," said Young. The word "sandlot" in the award's name represents a symbolic playground, where everyone enjoys doing life without a particular agenda. "We are looking for those who are serving above and beyond the call of duty," said Loiacono, "for students who take initiative to help the community—not because they have to, but because they want to."

Brianna Mercado was the first ever Justin Perkins Sandlot Hero award recipient. She received the award for volunteering with community organizations that help children. "Justin and I had the same doctor and probably had the same chemicals pumped through our veins," recalled Brianna. "He was a great guy and once I knew he passed away, I knew I wanted to stay involved in Sandlot Hero in every way I could. I am living Justin's dream. We want to inspire people to make changes in their community that matter. Changes that last."

"I found a calling by volunteering," said Brianna. "One of the first opportunities I took was at Camp Okizu. When I was a camper in 2007, Okizu gave me the strength and hope I needed to overcome my battle with cancer." Okizu remains an integral partner to children fighting cancer. "Without my Camp Okizu friends there were times that I felt ashamed and alone," Brianna continued. "Once I realized that there were so many others like me I became even stronger. The love that I received from the staff was overwhelming. I wanted to be just as loving as they were with me. Because of this I felt a need to give what I knew to other cancer fighters and their families."

John Bell and Dr. Michael "Mike" Amylon, a retired pediatric oncologist, created Camp Okizu from scratch. At the time, John volunteered at a hospice facility in Marin County where a friend of his died of cancer. His friend was in his forties and without kids of his own. This inspired John to create a program for young cancer patients.

Mike and other pediatric oncology doctors in the Bay Area attested to the need for this camp. A mutual friend suggested that John discuss his ideas with the oncology doctors, including Mike. They met and pooled common goals and interests to create a fledgling program with thirty children, hosted at a rented girls' camp near Sacramento.

John owned a travel agency in the Bay Area that helped fund the program and ultimately bought land to build a new facility. It quickly grew to accomodate two thousand five hundred campers a year—an expansive but modest resort dependent on the generosity of donors. No one has ever been turned away due to a lack of space as the programs and facilities continue growing. And it is always free to participants.

"My grandfather, who was Pennsylvania Dutch, believed in community. I can remember when the whole valley would come together to harvest each other's wheat fields. Maybe that is where my desire to give comes from," reflected John. "All I know is whenever I participated in the visualization exercise that gave the choice of carrying someone or being carried, I always pictured myself doing the carrying. I have always wanted to help."

Hundreds of campers each summer come to Okizu to escape the fears and frustrations of their illnesses. Programs also include camps for siblings of cancer victims who receive special attention that is otherwise directed to the sick child in the family. Okizu sponsors teens and twenties adventure getaways, family camps, and bereavement retreats for families who've lost a child for them to hold and help one another.

"Much of the evolution came simply from parents and others asking for help and us responding," explained John. "We saw or were asked to fill a need and created a program to do that. The sibling camp is an example. We operate the only camp we know of for brothers and sisters who suffer in different ways, but suffer nonetheless, along with the sick child."

"Camp has given me a certain confidence," shared a recent oncology camp participant. "I walk different, I am a lot more social, I am at peace at camp, not worried about anything, and I'm not scared of anything. To see what camp does, look at the children's faces. You don't see the scars, you don't see the pain, you see complete contentment." A younger camper wrote of his experience as well, "I miss camp so much and miss everyone. I have missed the smiles on all your faces and the songs we sing."

John Bell sinks into the back of a couch in a bright alcove just off the dining hall at Camp Okizu. A warm sun bounces off his shoulders and illuminates the room as campers enjoy a siesta on the decks next to their cabins. He tells the stories of families who have come and gone, of children who first came as campers, survived cancer, and now return year after year as counselors. People never really leave Camp Okizu and it never leaves them. He recalls a recent visit from a woman who first came to the camp in 1985. Her son and grandson are volunteers at Okizu to this day. John struggles to find the most meaningful out of a lifetime of memories but settles on one.

"One summer we had a twelve-year-old girl camper who was completely blind," said John. "Without being asked and with no one saying a word, other kids her age—who themselves were sick but not blind—took her by the hand and sat down with her over the first lunch. They cut her food; told her what was on her plate; helped her eat and ate with her; picked up her dishes; put them in the wash bins; and then walked outside arm-in-arm and down a path to their next adventure."

It is the courage and empathy of children that astonishes John most. "The kids are so brave and leave such a mark. To have them come back year after year is such an amazing feeling. For them to become volunteers to carry on the legacy is very humbling."

The volunteers—whether returning campers, college students, retired people or someone taking a week off from their job—are the backbone of the organization. And the benefactors who give so much make it all happen. "Without their donations and without the volunteers we would be lost," continued John. "We are all connected and I deeply feel that whenever I am here."

Brianna knows the power of this connection and the healing it brings to sick children. Now five years cancer-free, Brianna approaches a critical milestone. If treated early and aggressively with surgery and massive doses of radiation and chemotherapy, Ewing's Sarcoma victims have an over 70 percent survival rate past their fifth year of treatment.

In the year before heading on a celebratory European adventure with her sister, Brianna volunteered in the afternoons after her morning classes at University of California, Berkeley. Brianna also works at CoachArt, a nonprofit organization that offers classes and lessons in art and athletics to children with chronic and life-threatening illnesses and their siblings. For a few hours each month, CoachArt activities shift a child's focus away from the illness and toward another reason to live—inspiring them to achieve in violin lessons, voice coaching, soccer practice, or dance classes.

Today, Brianna teaches three young friends a few new fancy dance steps. They stand in front of a large mirror, spinning, talking, laughing, stretching, and reaching for the stars in an hour-long ballet lesson. At the end of the lesson they hug and set a date for the next class. Brianna is hopeful that her young dance students will feel well enough to kick up their heels at the next lesson. She knows progress on the dance floor and on the health front, and she understands how the last hour was a crucial reprieve for these young girls.

Based in Los Angeles since 2000, CoachArt sought to expand its programs to serve the youth of the Bay Area and pursued its new location in early 2011. CoachArt Regional Director Ashley Fontanetta supervised this operation. She set up an information table on the Berkeley campus to garner interest and volunteers and up walked Brianna.

Brianna embraced the CoachArt mission and spearheaded the creation of its Berkeley branch. "I believe it was because of her own personal experiences with life-threatening illnesses and dance that she immediately saw the value our programs bring to kids," said Ashley. "She is a natural leader who is highly respected because of her incandescence. She truly understands healing."

"I think Brianna's spirit has been with her all along; hers is as strong as I have ever felt in anybody," continued Ashley. "I don't think she realizes just how much she gives and means to people. She is kind and caring, and seems inexhaustible. Everyone who knows Brianna describes her the same. She never once questioned her disease, but used it to put hope in the hearts of others. Because of her kindness and dedication to helping others, the world is her oyster," said Ashley.

In addition to her class work toward a double major in dance and social welfare, and volunteer work at Camp Okizu and CoachArt, Brianna dances her heart out with friends who created Main Stacks, an award-winning hip-hop troupe. This twenty-one-year-old student was recently appointed as executive producer of the Northern California chapter of Prelude Urban Dance Competitions. Brianna also speaks at various engagements to high school students, encouraging them to live life to the fullest.

"We are all different because of her. Along with many others, I would not be the same person without her. She showed us strengths we did not know we had," shared Sabrina. Brianna and Sabrina's parents divorced when the twins were ten, and they did not speak to each other for years.

"Now, we can all laugh together in the same room. My family is closer and my life more rich because of Brianna and all that she went through. I think Brianna's main goal in life is to prove to everyone, every day, that the power of love is everything. She was like this before she got sick and is even more so today. She lives her life in a way to illustrate that care and compassion are all that matters," said Sabrina.

Brianna says she does not know which came first: her ease or disease. She does know that giving to others does not require any magical energy or battle with a life-threatening disease. With a little desire and a little time for a sick child in a hospital room, an impoverished family at a food bank, a senior citizen in a retirement facility, or someone who simply needs a hand with groceries, anyone can bring warmth to someone's world. Brianna's resilience and giving in this vein is profound:

> After being a year out of school, I returned with the pure motivation to live life to its fullest. I didn't look at my year off as a setback, but as a reason to step forward and begin my new journey as a survivor. While I was sick I was forced to find the light in every situation that I encountered.
>
> When you are stuck in a bed all day with nothing to do, you look for inspiration in the littlest of things. I danced when I could, visited my teammates at school, and loved interaction with people. This just motivated me more to get better. This is what got me through the tough times.
>
> I always keep an image in the back of my mind of the children I met in the hospital. I know how badly they had wanted to be living a healthy life again. I volunteer for this reason and a thousand others, all based in the natural desire to share love and make lives

better. What I get back is immeasurable. We should all be bringing positive change to the world—not to fulfill a requirement or to improve a resume—but simply because it's what we should do.

In a schedule crammed with classes and homework, kids to play with, dance shows to train for, and friends and family to spend time with, Brianna added one more thing. She joined Big or Bigger, an action-oriented organization that utilizes social media and community to improve society. Brianna organized and facilitated the Berkeley Dance for Cancer events to provide awareness and fundraising for various cancer research and treatment organizations.

"Several hundred dancers came together. We raised just under two thousand dollars with this event," said Brianna. She also created the BriPositive Challenge to help people have fun, live their dreams, and passionately share their goodness with the world. The challenge encourages others to dance like no one is watching, join the bone marrow registry, watch the sunrise, and give blood. People from around the world have embraced Brianna's suggestions.

"About things I want to do, I always ask myself: 'If not now, when?'" Brianna said. "Then I take action right away." In the spirit of John Bell, Brianna Mercado, Becky, and so many others, everyone should apply urgency in their quest to help others. Now is the time to make the world a better place.

FUNDING CHILDHOOD CANCER RESEARCH

On average, every high school in America has two students diagnosed with cancer. It is the leading cause of death among children under the age of fifteen. Every day thirty-six children or adolescents are diagnosed with this disease.

Today, the rate of cancer among children is increasing faster than any other age group except those over age sixty-five. The causes of childhood cancer are unknown and thus most preventive measures are unavailable.

While medical research and new treatments for childhood cancer are vastly under-funded, there are organizations dedicated to helping cancer patients win their battles. Many are small grassroots programs. Camp Okizu, CoachArt and Sparrow Clubs are examples.

These entities give victims and their families financial support, periods of joy, shoulders to cry on, education, and much more. Other national entities assist by sharing information, funding, and providing actual medical care for young cancer victims, like Alex's Lemonade Stand Foundation.

Alexandra "Alex" Scott was first diagnosed with cancer at the age of two. In the ensuing years, she fought the disease and built a lemonade stand at age four to raise money for other pediatric cancer patients. She said she wanted to give the money to doctors to "help other kids, like they helped me."

Her first stand raised two thousand dollars and more money each subsequent year. Before she died at age eight, her organization raised over one million dollars for cancer research.

News of this brave girl's efforts circulated the world, and people collected local funds with their own stands to give to what is now a national organization. From this poignant beginning, the foundation has raised millions more dollars for childhood cancer research.

Since 2006, Alex's Lemonade

Stand Foundation has provided over two hundred grants to doctors and institutions creating diagnostic and curative measures to fight childhood cancer.

Dozens of private organizations diligently generate income to fund cancer research and patient care. Top-rated nonprofits—those directly funding research instead of advertising and director's salaries—include the National Cancer Coalition, The National Comprehensive Cancer Care Network, and Alex's Lemonade Stand.

These organizations collectively provide hundreds of millions of critical dollars to childhood cancer research. However, the federal government still provides the lion's share of research funding.

The National Cancer Institute (NCI) is the U.S. government's primary agency for cancer research and training. Approximately half of the NCI budget is allocated to research grants awarded to scientists who work at local hospitals and universities.

More than 6,500 research grants are now funded at more than 150 cancer centers and specialized research facilities located in 49 states. In 2010, NCI was provided 5.1 billion dollars from the federal government.

NCI is an agency in the National Institutes of Health. The NIH is funded and directed through the Department of Health and Human Services, which operated with a budget of 78.7 billion dollars in 2010. By comparison, the Department of Defense had a budget of 663.7 billion dollars.

Cancer research receives only a small portion of the Health and Human Service budget, less than 1 percent of the monies dedicated to the military and related industries. This ratio is troubling. It can only be adjusted by the political will of the people to direct lawmakers' priorities.

For Justin Perkins, Brianna Mercado, and the thousands who suffer each year, it is prudent to work toward cancer cures through research. Two primary actions are needed: donate to causes that treat and improve the lives of those suffering from childhood cancer, and contact lawmakers about the need to create a more philanthropic budget.

CHANGING THE WORLD BY CHANGING YOUR INFORMATION SOURCES

Justin Perkins and Sandlot Hero are regularly mentioned in a small, community-driven Internet newsletter called the Cupertino Patch, which is part of the national Patch network.

In twenty-three states and dozens of towns across America, this national media service with local editorial control is an excellent resource for objective and balanced reporting in its respective regions.

Patch succeeds as a "community-specific news and information platform dedicated to providing comprehensive and trusted local coverage for individual towns and communities."

There are thousands of alternative news sources from which to choose. As the American public is inundated by main stream media networks and cable television news, alternative news blogs and websites proliferate (Goodnews network.com, Happynews.com, and Wikinews.org are a few).

While Patch has experienced an interesting evolution from a small local conglomerate to a national corporate operation, it maintains local editorial control.

Justin Perkins wanted to make a difference in people's lives after he was gone. Through Sandlot Hero and the people it salutes, his dreams are coming true.

The reporting on Sandlot Hero's positive impact—by a news source that highlights collective and individual good—allows Justin's legacy to thrive. Choosing responsible information sources empowers honest media outlets with greater force in our society.

ERIC PLANTENBERG

Introspection

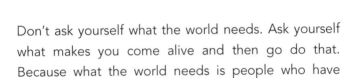

Don't ask yourself what the world needs. Ask yourself what makes you come alive and then go do that. Because what the world needs is people who have come alive.

—HOWARD THURMAN

I thank Eric for giving me my freedom.

—RON ROSS

Eric Plantenberg and his bride, Michelle, were just beginning their three-year honeymoon when they walked into a language school in downtown Cairo. One of their intentions in this round-the-globe trip was to study abroad. Learning Arabic in Egypt met that goal. They settled in at the Drayah Language Center for three months of learning to speak the native tongue.

While living in Cairo, Eric and Michelle walked streets painted with Egypt's economic disparity. The upper echelon of society spoke English and drove Mercedes while the poor and homeless did neither. Orphanages peppered the city and

Cairo's poor—especially the kids—moved Eric and Michelle. The honeymoon goal of taking a few years to travel the world allowed them several weeks in Cairo. This was long enough for Eric and Michelle to get a true sense of what life as an underprivileged Egyptian meant, and to create a program for change.

Orphaned children in Egypt wake each morning in barrack-style bedrooms to the same simple breakfast. They move to classrooms with feeble desks and paint-chipped walls and later to asphalt playgrounds behind towering cement walls. Dirty heads, seeking eyes, and yearning souls peek around corners to the outside world.

Although most children in these orphanages arrived without formed ideals or memories of another way of life, they innately long for a mother's tender heart and a father's gentle hand. Almost without exception, each child remains an orphan until old enough to live independently, with or without the necessary tools to succeed. Over time they realize life should have been different, and a feeling of emptiness creeps in. An orphan's bedtime is especially hard as innocent spirits grieve the loneliness and despair.

After a month in Egypt and a grasp on the language, Eric and Michelle thought they could help. "I began to believe that a key to success and a ticket out of poverty in Egypt was to speak English," said Eric.

"I brought the idea to create English classes for underprivileged kids to the head instructor at Drayah, but he said there were too many children and not enough space at the facility to take on a broad scale program. I realized that we did not need to help a million kids to change the world, but maybe we could teach just one and that would change the lives of others in Egypt."

The Plantenbergs had enough seed money to fund a program accessible to a few kids at a time. The plan was simple and they started the school.

In the summer of 2006 the school began teacher interviews. Each teacher was responsible for recruiting his or her own students. Typically, a group of students were taught at Drayah in ninety-minute sessions, three days a week, coupled with their regular schooling. The average annual pay per teacher at this school was two hundred fifty dollars, a larger compensation than Cairo public school teachers' salaries. U.S. dollars yielded a lot at this rate.

After returning to the U.S., Eric and Michelle monitored the progress of the school with monthly profit and loss statements and teacher reports. Over one hundred students attended in the first year. The second year was dedicated to sustaining the program numbers before expanding. The Drayah management faced teacher protests in the third year, with demands for autonomy and kinder management. This threatened the program as it eliminated the primary classroom location.

One teacher, then another, took what they knew to the orphanages. Teachers requested onsite classroom space to enrich lives and orphanage directors gladly obliged. Today, Egypt's poorest students are empowered by the English language, a skill that will change their lives. Maybe the one child Eric dreamt of helping is among them, poised to change the future of Egypt.

Eric has a history of helping others to help themselves. His experience as a mentor began in 1996, when he and his partner Roger Seip founded a personal and business improvement company, Freedom Personal Development. In the past they sold books door-to-door and became sales trainers for different companies, until joining forces again to start their business. Today, they facilitate personal growth through group seminars and retreats. They inspire others to grow by example.

Freedom Personal Development's core philosophies are embraced by thousands. They focus on a single outcome: to discover and utilize greater personal freedoms to make the world a better place. The company's astronomical growth reflects the success of its teachings; their gross revenue has averaged nearly 50 percent annual increases since its inception.

At a recent Freedom Personal Development seminar, Eric stood in front of a full conference hall. A few people knew him and said hello, while others filtered anonymously into open seats. The white-collar men and women, mostly in their thirties and forties, scanned the room or the cover of the packet before them. Eric addressed the group with a simple admission.

"I'm not here to talk about me, I am here to talk about you." With a welcoming, clear voice Eric invited each guest into the business of the day. He commended their respective desires for improvement and moved like a purposeful hiker toward a distant peak, with serene focus. His words flowed from an open heart and curious mind, both postures he encouraged for the group. On an enthusiastic and mystifying four-hour journey with Eric, many were mentally guided to a new state-of-mind.

People sat motionless in chairs, eyes closed to let their minds wander. They paired up in quiet exercises to share dreams, nightmares, laughter, and tears. The commonplace work and life conversations revealed a meaningful thread, as many found the switch to turn on their lives. In three subsequent seminars over the next two months, Eric gave the participants tools to use that switch.

Ron Ross has known Eric for several years, as a student and good friend of his. Eric's trademark expression to "Be Free" is one Ron knows well. "Those are his parting words at the end of his speaking engagements, those words are on his voice mail greetings, and in his e-mail signature. At first I just thought it was a cute catch phrase with little substance."

"My entire worldview was changed when I fully understood Eric's teachings that 'I get to choose.' I used to think I was hostage to the world around me," continued Ron. "I realized that no matter what the circumstances or events are, I still get to choose my attitude, my behavior and actions, my demeanor. I never have to be fearful, angry, bitter, or sad unless I choose that, and I am *free* to not choose that."

Across America there are dozens of personal development companies, hundreds of personal development trainers, and thousands of self-help books available to make your life better. The measure of success in this industry is not the number of people you make feel good or desire change; it's the ones who actually do change.

Improving communication with partners and children, embracing personal health and fitness, using passion as a life compass, and being compassionate to yourself and others, rank high on Eric's priority list for change. It is the collective positive difference all of these make in the world that matters most to him. Growth and success come more readily for those who inspire through action, who lead by example and who stand on their own principles. Eric's principles caught up with him in yet another distant spot of the world, after he started the English language school for orphans.

In the spring of 2011, Eric Plantenberg sought the top of the world. His goal to climb as high as he safely could culminated at the summit of Mt. Everest. For seven years Eric and his mountaineering partner and friend Scott Patch prepared for Everest, and experienced the challenges of big mountain expeditions by climbing some of the world's tallest peaks.

They summited Alaska's 20,328-foot Mt. Denali, Tibet's 26,864-foot Cho Oyu and others, to hone skills and gain confidence for Everest. His expedition was in some part for personal gain and reward, but more to emphasize the need to educate young people, especially girls, in Pakistan. The trip featured a pledge program for his organization, We Climb for Kids, to fund the building of schoolhouses in remote Central Asia.

Climbing Mt. Everest was on Eric's to-do list for years, well before his daughter Mae was conceived. She was born, an adventure all her own, to two joyful and proud parents. Michelle understood and selflessly supported Eric's Everest dream, despite the risks involved. On the eve of the expedition they celebrated Eric honoring his commitment with their happy and healthy one-year-old daughter. Ironically, Eric's climb to help youngsters halfway across the world would estrange him from his own little girl.

After weeks in the Himalayas acclimating and moving gear from Base Camp to alpine ledges, Eric's team neared the peak. Eric straddled the icy ridge on Everest's highest shoulder, nearly six miles above sea level. After several hours in the dark, inching toward the heavens and through the death zone, dawn arrived on the summit push for him and climbing partner, Lakpa Sherpa.

Since midnight they had scaled vertical pitches of ice and rock and tiptoed with sharp crampon cleats across ledges narrower than a hand's-breadth in the most perilous sections. Less than a mile from the top of the world, Eric braced against the frigid wind and gathered energy for his next step. The bright white ridge contoured the sky before him and as he surveyed the remaining distance to the peak, something caught his eye. Eric noticed another's climbing rope as it dangled loose off a ridge fifty yards ahead.

He blinked twice to clear his head and tried to take another struggled breath of supplemental oxygen. Eric was operating on less than 50 percent of his sea-level oxygen intake. Each inhale is precious at thirty thousand feet and brings just enough critical oxygen for another small advance uphill until the next ineffective breath. His heart sank when he realized the dangling rope was not a figment of his oxygen-starved brain, but an indication that someone was in trouble.

In the final reaches of Mt. Everest expeditions, climbers undergo a slow death as the lack of oxygen and extreme cold steal vitality inch-by-inch. Above twenty-five thousand feet, in the death zone, survival is a numbers game as the body uses oxygen faster than it can be replenished.

According to *National Geographic*, "Climbers who venture

into this zone cannot escape the potentially deadly effects of oxygen deprivation; they can only attempt to minimize and control what breathing the thin air at high altitudes does to their bodies." This is why climbers do not sleep, eat, or move well in the final days leading up to the summit. The body conserves all systems and is on overdrive just to keep the heart beating. On summit day, the mind pushes the body to its ultimate limits, sometimes too far.

In 2011, the Adventure Stats website claimed that 207 people have died on Everest. Since the mountain was first officially climbed in 1953, an average of three to four people per year die climbing. Statistically, those who have legitimately attempted to summit are approximately one twelve-thousandth of a percent of the population on earth. Decimally speaking, this is 0.0012 percent. Those who make it to the top are an even smaller category. More people have won medals in a single summer Olympics than have successfully reached the top of Mt. Everest.

Adventure opportunities, like rafting remote and wild rivers or climbing the world's highest and most dangerous peaks, are available to virtually everyone. The most seasoned alpinists and those with little experience led by specialized tour companies simultaneously share a mountain in pursuit of the summit.

Several outfits lead guided tours on Mt. Everest. While most require clients to have significant mountaineering experience, others are not as stringent. People with minimal alpine skills and seventy thousand dollars can sign up for the summit package and defer to professional leaders for most of the trip's responsibilities. While the physical demands are extreme, the professional guides and Sherpas shoulder most of the logistical, technical, and mental load.

Eric, his Sherpa, "Patch" and the rest of the expedition team members comprised enough experience to do this trip as an unguided expedition. The team spent two months in Tibet slowly moving up the shoulder of the mountain to transport gear, gain physical and mental strength, and become acclimatized for the push to the summit.

For weeks, Everest climbers take many up and down trips to the highest camps, each above fifteen thousand feet. However, it is the last three days that are the most rigorous and draining. A post to the We Climb For Kids Facebook page depicts the physical challenges of this feat.

In the 72 hours surrounding their summit day, Scott and Eric slept a total of 4 hours and consumed less than 1400 calories—in that same 3-day period they climbed for 27 hours. And that doesn't account for all the energy spent packing and unpacking camps, getting snow for cooking or water, and the many hours sitting around freezing in the death zone.

There are essentially two routes to the top of the world: the south and the north. Both are fraught with deadly challenges and neither has a good scorecard. Between the years 2000 and 2006 approximately five thousand climbers attempted to reach the top of Mt. Everest. Two-thirds failed to summit or died upon the return to Base Camp.

The final push to the top of Everest from the northeast

side includes three sections known as the First, Second, and Third Steps. This grueling two-mile stretch from the final high-altitude camp to the summit and back can take up to sixteen hours. Climbers typically begin the trek at midnight.

The Second Step is considered the most challenging of the three. Life-threatening elements define this reach: fatigue from weeks of climbing; exposure to very high winds; significant slope and variation of gully, ice, snow, and rock face; an inches-wide ridge to traverse a cliff with no end in sight; and a rickety forty-year-old vertical ladder.

Climbers must scale all of this in the dead of night with crampon spikes on frozen boots and narrow-beam head-lamps, to ascend a deadly one-hundred-foot wall at an over twenty-eight-thousand-foot altitude. The mountain exacts a cost to reach her summit. This small section of the climb can take over an hour. A slip can easily mean death.

Eric Simonson and Jochen Hemmleb described this pitch in their article on the expedition that investigated the fate of early Everest pioneer George Mallory, who died on the North-east Ridge:

> The initial climb up the Second Step itself involves a 10-foot-high slab to the right of a narrow chimney, surmounted by way of a narrow ramp and a short rock step interspersed with ledges. A prominent snow patch, some 23 to 30 feet high and lying at an angle of 50 degrees, leads up to the foot of the final 16-foot headwall. During the first confirmed ascent in 1960 this was climbed by a crack on its left side.

The 1975 Chinese expedition placed a ladder on this pitch which is now commonly used for the ascent. While the ladder is only 15 feet high, it is dead vertical and tends to move while climbers ascend it. From the top rung of the ladder, a tricky mantle move onto a ledge leads to easier terrain below the top of the Second Step and close to the crest of the Northeast Ridge. At this point the exposure is incredible, with the entire North face at your feet, literally 10,000 feet of exposure.

It was just after negotiating the Second Step and before the Third that Eric and Lakpa Sherpa realized that the literal lifeline shared by the earlier group of climbers disappeared straight down from the razor ridge. Breathlessly, he and Lakpa reached the other team attached to that rope and together they struggled to bring the fallen climber back up. It was John Delaney, a fellow climber Eric befriended during the weeks spent at Base Camp.

Hand over hand they pulled the rope to retrieve John, who was unresponsive and lifeless. After several breathless minutes of hauling him up to the precipice ridge they saw what each had feared. Hoping for a miracle, they asked John's team to inject him with the stimulant epinephrine for a futile last shot at life. Eric and Lakpa signaled each other that he was dying and knew there was nothing more to do.

John, a successful Irish businessman, talked frequently with Eric during their months on the mountain. On his first attempt at the mountain years earlier, John failed to reach the summit. He was determined to succeed on this expedition. His wife and soulmate understood and blessed his need to climb it again. At Base Camp, Eric and John shared stories of their children and the worries of leaving little loved ones behind to accomplish cherished goals. John was a father of three, but he did not know his youngest child and only daughter. She was born just two days before his death, with John unaware of her birth.

Many Everest climbers choose not to help a fallen comrade. The summit is a counterbalance of ambition and values. One always tips the scale in the end. Eric and Lakpa did what they could, paid their respects to John, and continued on the final reach to the summit. The bodies of those who die at this altitude remain on the mountain forever, as John's does.

As the sun rose, Eric was seven hours into his final climb of the ten-week expedition. One very long hour on the Third Step and summit ridge remained. Each step was followed by a forever pause to take five halting breaths as deep as he could to summon dying strength.

This cycle repeated endlessly in the final hour. Eric and his team willed themselves forward, and made it to the peak. Cold and weary, Eric scanned the panorama of mountain and sky from the highest possible point on earth. He saluted his team and the moment with three quick pictures and started back down.

The need to reach the summit a couple of hours into daylight is historically evident. There is a very narrow window of time to summit and descend on the actual summit day. Any delays from weather, equipment failure, human bottlenecks at critical climb points, or other factors can be fatal. It is only at a return to Advance Base Camp, several hours and thousands of feet below, that achievement is celebrated. Here, Eric humbly toasted success and precious life.

What is a man made of who climbs to the top of the world and who leads thousands of willing participants to reach their own personal heights? Discipline and drive. Eric rode in his grandfather's lap on tractors before he was old enough to walk. As a youngster, he woke up at 4:30 a.m. on summer mornings to work and finished the day at dusk. As a college student when he sold books door-to-door and he heard "no" infinitely more times than "yes".

Thereafter, Eric helped grow a national pet treat business from two hundred to two thousand outlets in only nine months by improving sales techniques among store staff. A client shared with Eric that his presentation to the sales team was the best he had ever seen. Freedom Personal Development was the culmination of Eric's desire to help people improve their lives.

Eric's values and work ethic came early in life. His grandfather had a particularly strong influence. "My grandfather, Pappy, was my first hero. Raising beef cattle and hogs on 360 acres near Dell Rapids, South Dakota, his life revolved around farming," recalled Eric. "He was born on a farm, married and raised his family on a farm, and after 66 years of pushing a plow, he retired from the farm. He wasn't financially wealthy or famous, although he was loved and respected by those that knew him."

Eric's grandfather exemplified respect, hard work and life

in the moment; even thirty years later he gleans wisdom from that man. Eric recalled one life lesson in particular from Pappy:

I spent part of the summer of 1976 on the farm. It was the worst drought in recorded history. Even as a youngster, I could feel the tension throughout the community. There was no water for crops so there were no crops for money. Doubt led to deep concern and concern rose to fear, as farmers all around worried about their future.

One evening as Pappy and I finished the chores of feeding the cattle, we walked to the edge of the cornfield. It was blistering hot. The crops were burning up. Pappy looked out across the field from below the brim of his Zip Feed hat, with his hands in his overall pockets.

"This is the driest summer I can remember," was all he said. While others were predicting and stressing over doomsday scenarios, sadly reflecting on the good ole' days, or worried about their future, he was only making an observation as he worked with what he had.

Pappy lived in the moment. He lived judgment free as far as I could tell, and was apparently unattached to concern. His comment, which means so much to me now, was simply an expression of awareness of the here and now, which is how he always seemed to live.

The few words of an old farmer many years ago ring as poetry to Eric's ears. "That one comment, that one brief living example of that truth, has meant more to me than a thousand written pages ever could."

The power of Eric's thoughts and emotional energy is from living in the moment. He believes a mindset controlled by positive internal input and how you perceive your situation achieves fulfillment. "I would rather be at peace in an awful environment than in turmoil in paradise," he reflected. A conscious choice to watch, listen and read what encourages success is a cornerstone of Eric's philosophy.

Eric's definition of failure is "believing that what happened wasn't the best thing that could have happened." Eric believes it is fundamental to embrace reality and to know that situations you are in today may have no bearing on where you are going. This is not to discount the past or to live in the future. It does not mean that challenges will disappear with positive thinking.

On a very basic level, Eric believes that it is important to take a break from thinking that reality should be different from what it is and to simultaneously believe in your abilities. (See article page 209.) In other words, love what is and trust in yourself.

Regarding achievement, Eric said, "Success is really tiny, incremental improvements that move you toward your goal." This understanding and approach allows the opportunity to measure progress, take time to celebrate large and small achievements, and create a purpose-filled life lived moment by moment to improve your world and the world at large.

After years of refining personal development curriculum and following his dream to help people realize theirs, Eric created the Abundant Living Retreat, a place of solitude and relaxation from the daily grind. The essence of the retreat is to reconnect people with their hopes and passions through reflection. Though this workshop, Eric teaches that the present is a place of rich abundance and the place for self-awareness that embraces possibility.

At the Abundant Living Retreat, participant Mirabelle Hagger shared her experience. "In four days, I experienced so many shifts in every aspect of my life—deep healing on many levels—and felt the floodgates of gratitude open in my heart. I learned to love myself and a room full of people I had never met before with compassion, honesty and openness," she said. "It was the most life-changing four days I have ever experienced. I would say that I finally feel in charge of my life."

The retreat encourages people to release things that weigh them down, to loosen their grip and let it be. "I just feel free. I feel like I can do anything," shared participant Roselyn Martinez. "I have never laughed so much," stated Hector Duenas, his gratitude striking a consistent chord. "Thank you, Eric, for changing my life forever."

Eric Plantenberg is a man of innumerable accomplishments. He built a multi-million dollar company from scratch, completed four Ironman triathlons, kayaked the Zambezi River and he started a language school for children in Egypt. He married a beautiful woman who is building her own dynamic business and is the mother of a precious baby girl, who looks a lot like her dad. He and Michelle now have a son on the way. Eric raised tens of thousands of dollars for schoolhouse construction in Pakistan in pledge money from his Mt.

Everest climb. According to Michelle, "The crazy thing is, he thinks all of this is normal."

Ron Ross shared more of Freedom Personal Development's inspirational philosophy. "A cornerstone to Eric's philosophy and teaching is 'What you see is what you get, and what you see is what you look for.' When I finally understood that principle I simply began to look for good people, good things, opportunities, positive relationships. This is what I got. It is powerful and life-changing. I thank Eric for giving me my freedom."

This book is partly an outcome of Eric's teachings. As a long-time believer in the conscious and systematic pursuit of dreams, I sat in Eric's seminar described above. My life was incredibly rich as an international river guide, owner of a global adventure travel company, husband to the most amazing woman I know, and father to lovely kids. Yet, in the two years that preceded Eric's seminar, I felt as though I was stumbling and pursued less than noble goals.

After nearly twenty years in the river guide outfitting industry, I gave that up. My focus shifted to making lots of money to provide what I thought was best for my young family. As a commercial real estate broker, my profession brought rewards but was not spiritually fulfilling. Nor was it a job that employed my gifts and passions. As a result, I had numbed myself to what I really wanted from life.

As it grew increasingly obvious that my goal to get wealthy wouldn't bring me happiness, I searched for solutions. My life was no longer about helping people experience joy, adventure, camaraderie, and confidence as an international adventure outfitter. Something was missing. I was sleepwalking through my professional life and largely through Eric's brilliant guidance, I woke up.

Most of the awakening came via the Abundant Living Retreat. When I engaged with Eric's work I left grateful, aware, energized, and empowered. When daily difficulties appear or large concerns drag me down, I get still in that moment to really understand and accept the issue. From this state, my all-encompassing energy and spirit can exist in acceptance and joy. *Courage creates change.* Love is unrestrained. Passion and compassion emerge as beacon and compass, and the energy of the world is raised.

Eric Plantenberg lifts others up. From the tops of mountains to the quiet of desert retreats, he inspires people to make themselves and the world a better place. He illustrates how courage—in the form of introspection and generosity—is a fulcrum to a rich and meaningful life.

LOVING WHAT IS

In her seminal work, *Loving What Is*, Byron Katie unfolds a simple but effective process for living life. It is her belief, and one that Eric Plantenberg ascribes to, that your thoughts get in the way of personal freedom. She comes by this assessment honestly.

In the 1980s, Katie experienced a period of deep depression. She found herself on the floor in a halfway house in a fetal position of emotional, mental, and spiritual devastation. She reached her breaking point in a battle against abject depression and disillusionment. When she realized that her own debilitating thoughts drove this process, her enlightenment to their existence would lead her out.

Katie calls her form of inquiry "The Work." It is a systematic best-practice for instantaneous inquiry into thoughts that drive you crazy or make you stressed. The four question process is a powerful tool to move from a life of subjective awareness to one of objective awareness. It is her belief that most thoughts ultimately disregard reality and block the powerful freedoms that come when you love what *is*.

The Work investigates the underlying thoughts that distract us from reality. When we have a thought or judgment about others or ourselves, Katie encourages self-dialogue through four simple questions:

1. *Is the thought true?*
2. *Can I absolutely know it is true?*
3. *How do I react, what happens, when I believe that thought?*
4. *Who would I be without that thought?*

Katie does not suggest ignoring a thought but investigating it to the root cause. Each question is designed not to remove the thought or push it out of your head, but to examine and understand it. Through this posture of inquiry the weight of attachment to negative thoughts is lifted and reality becomes a beacon.

AFTERWORD

From caring comes courage.

—LAO TZU

Courage reveals purpose.

—UNKNOWN

After half a century on earth, I realize that I am here simply to enjoy moments in an ongoing attempt at a life of benevolent purpose. Learning from and writing about the great people in this book helped me to recognize this.

In the two years I spent researching and writing *The Gift of Courage*, I grew much closer to my friend Kelley Kalafatich. She is the reason I decided to write this book in the first place. Thirty years ago Kelley became an inspirational role model and a great encourager to me. Everyone who meets Kelley finds a hidden treasure, and I tell her story as a gesture of gratitude and love.

I also came to know and love Jim Adams, Josh Kern and Thurgood Marshall Academy, Martha Ryan, Judy Crawford, Carrie Hamilton and Homeless Prenatal Program, Jeff Leeland and Sparrow Clubs, Dennis Guthrie, Brianna Mercado, and Eric Plantenberg. Thank you all for bringing your gifts into this world. My children have role models because of you. The philosophies and organizations you represent are detailed at the end of each chapter to salute your actions that are improving our world. I hope this book honors each of your stories and reflects the goodness you bring into your communities. By living your calling you inspire and elevate us all.

I believe that each of us has a unique purpose or calling. Many intuitively know this big "why." My wife Danielle is one. She is here to love and care for those around her and to genuinely spread joy. Finding my purpose was much harder and took deep courage.

From the early 1980s through the first few years of the twenty-first century I was an international river guide, a manager of an adventure travel company in Norway, and an owner of a large outfitting business that ran global wilderness adventure trips in Alaska, California, Hawaii, Oregon, Iceland, Mexico, Idaho, Bolivia, and Norway. Then I traded in my Tevas for neck ties to be a good father, which I thought meant earning lots of money, among other things. Getting rich became my primary driver and paradoxically our financial situation became very bleak. Except for time spent with my family, I was unfulfilled and lost. My life felt like an oxymoron. I wasn't me. I sat at work frustrated and unmotivated, lay in bed at night distraught by debt and paralyzed by emptiness and went for long, introspective walks every day before my kids woke up. I knew I could do better, and do more.

I asked a lot of questions of those who had found or were also seeking greater purpose in their lives, including many very notable people. I attended personal development retreats and read book after book about those who had sought and discovered their life's meaning. I also asked a lot of questions about myself. I took time to inquire about my thoughts, understand my deep feelings and fears, and focus on what brought me joy.

Little by little, I did more of what made me feel fulfilled. This awoke buried memories as I traveled back to a time of innocence and happiness. I remembered being the only junior high kid who organized backpacking trips for dear classmates who wanted to explore wilderness and enjoy silence in the company of true friends. I recalled running a rafting company in my twenties and crying tears of joy one evening after a young guide I had trained took his first group of paying clients down a wild river. Afterward, he exclaimed to me "Today, my dream came true!" I thought of the days in my early thirties when I taught high school students in bush Alaska to use gumption and creativity in their thoughts and actions.

I began to feel and know why I was here. This was validated just a few weeks ago as I marveled at my nine-year-old son Dawson, when he took deep, soulful breaths between sentences as he explained the connection, purpose, pride and love he felt when helping a young classmate with a learning disability to complete math and reading worksheets.

I peeled back the layers of my heart to find its core. I rediscovered what made it sing in all parts of my life. I realized that serving others and sharing stories of individual and community achievement was infinitely more rewarding than just chasing the dollar. Writing *The Gift of Courage* made this clear to me. I found and now humbly let my unique personal strengths and passions direct me. With modesty, my purpose is to help anyone—even you—use deep courage to embrace fears and open your heart to find meaning in life. I discovered mine through the help of loved ones and caring mentors who showed me a path. I want to pay this forward by sharing what I learned. I want to help others find their own personal greatness.

How do I know I am living my purpose? As I wrote this book and as I pen others, including *The Courage Compass: An Essential Guide to Finding Your Meaning and Purpose*, and when I speak to individuals and groups about how to realize true meaning in their lives, time stands still, my heart is full and I feel an indescribable grace-filled energy wash over and through me. This also happens when I drift down a peaceful river or marvel at my kids' bliss and wonder. I am wholly gratified in these moments as I do what I am meant to do. And my life is not perfect. Sometimes problems cloud purpose, frustration trumps serenity, and sadness overwhelms happiness. Through it all, I still live my dreams.

Danielle and our kids, Dari, Delaney, and Dawson give me pause every day. I am blessed by their love and I write about great people and good deeds for them. My greatest joy is to watch my kids laugh and to laugh with them. Just yesterday we laughed so hard that Dari, one of my six-year-old twin daughters, said she had "run out of laughs" and then we laughed some more. My greatest comfort is lying in bed with my arms around Danielle, knowing this gives her comfort too. We have done this for twenty years and it is still the best feeling in the world.

We feel blessed to live in Central Oregon, a wide-open stretch of country nestled into the largest piece of undeveloped land in the contiguous U.S. This area spans parts of Oregon,

Idaho, California, and Nevada. If you look at the "Earth at Night" poster, it reveals this region as the darkest part of the lower 48. Redmond, a town of twenty-five thousand, sits on the western edge of this expanse known as the Great Basin. We live just outside of Redmond amid ranch lands with endless views of the nearby ten-thousand-foot Three Sisters Mountains. Starry skies filled with universal glory, forever Cascade panoramas, and a community of warm and caring people makes our hometown heaven on earth.

There are so many in my community to thank for their guidance and love as I wrote this book. My mom, Nancy Gregori, was my first-rate editor. With a PhD in Education and decades as a teacher and public school administrator, she used her credentials to edit these pages as they came off the ink-jet printer. She literally read each chapter over twenty times, one version and one sentence at a time. She is also my kids' precious caregiver. Thanks, Mom.

Lynn Schooler was another invaluable editor and resource. I am very grateful for our two decades of friendship and our travels to distant corners of the earth together. His books, including *The Blue Bear* and *Walking Home*, are award-winning bestsellers that showcase the beauty of Alaska and the blessing of personal discovery. Lynn showed me how to be a better writer by editing and restructuring my words with patience and prodding.

Lauren Ruef polished *The Gift of Courage* into its final state. She is a talented writer and editor who combs through sentences and words with a skill and artistry that belies her youth. Katherine Lloyd gave the book a treasured typeset, and graphic arts genius Russ McIntosh made the cover shine with the book's essence. Thanks to each of you.

My friends Bob Platt, Laurie Rice, Emmet Lucey, Kathi Keller, Mirabelle Hagger, and Keith Bunney were also helpful; I am blessed to know them. I also love that Bob lives on our property and shares his strengths with our family. I also thank my sister, brother, step-mom, in-laws, nieces and nephews, teachers, and other friends who've graced my life and taught me so much.

I wrote *The Gift of Courage* to show the rewards of a meaningful life for each person individually and for the communities touched by regular yet extraordinary people who live their dreams. A portion of the book's proceeds covers rehabilitation and therapy expenses for people you've read about, scholarships for children, and donations to other worthy causes. With the purchase of this book, you are helping richly deserving people. Thank you for being a part of this community.

Made in the USA
San Bernardino, CA
07 October 2013